Do Brilliantly

AS Psychology

Mike Cardwell

Claire Meldrum

Jane Willson

Series Editor: Jayne de Courcy

Contents

How this book will help you
by Mike Cardwell, Claire Meldrum and Jane Willson

This book will help you to improve your performance in the AQA (Specification A) AS level Psychology exam. This specification for Psychology has six topics, organized into three modules. Each topic is split into 'subsections'. For example, 'Stress' is divided into 'Stress as a bodily response' and 'Sources of stress'. Each of these topics (except for 'Research Methods') is also accompanied by a '**critical issue**', which covers an aspect of the topic that is an important application of that topic. For example, an application of 'Human memory' is 'Eye-witness testimony'.

The topics covered by your AQA–A specification

The AQA–A topics, subsections and critical issues (plus appropriate chapters in this book) are as follows:

Topic	Critical Issue	*Do Brilliantly* Chapter number
MODULE 1		
Human memory ● Short-term and long-term memory ● Forgetting	Eye-witness testimony	1
Attachments in development ● The development and variety of attachments ● Deprivation and privation	Day care	2
MODULE 2		
Stress ● Stress as a bodily response ● Sources of stress	Stress management	3
Abnormality ● Defining psychological abnormality ● Biological and psychological models of abnormality	Eating disorders	4
MODULE 3		
Social influence ● Conformity and minority influence ● Obedience to authority	Ethical issues	5
Research methods ● Qualitative and quantitative research methods ● Research design and implementation ● Data analysis	–	6

Exam practice – how to answer questions better

Students frequently fail to perform as well as they might in exams because they have poor **exam skills** or cannot apply what they know effectively. This is evident from how surprised many students are when they receive an exam grade that bears little relation to the amount of work they have done in preparation for the exam.

To get a good grade in AS level Psychology you need a good grasp of the subject matter and good exam technique. Your main textbook will help you to develop your knowledge and understanding. **This book can help you improve your exam technique, so that you can make the most effective use of what you know**.

Each of the six chapters in this book (relating to the six sections of the AQA–A AS level Psychology specification) is broken down into five separate elements. Each chapter has the following sections:

1 Exam Questions and 'Choosing the best question'

Each chapter starts with two typical exam questions of the sort you will find on a real AQA–A AS level Psychology paper. In your exam (except for the Research Methods questions), you will only be expected to answer one of these two questions. The '**Choosing the best question**' section shows you what to look for when reading through the questions and helps you **select the question that is likely to yield most marks for you**.

2 Students' Answers and 'How to score full marks'

For one of the exam questions we provide two **typical students' answers**. These answers show many of the **most common mistakes** that students make under exam conditions, but also how well-prepared students can deal effectively with the time constraints of an exam question.

The students' answers are followed by a section called '**How to score full marks**'. This shows you where and how the answers could be improved, e.g. we explain exactly what the question is asking for; we point out missing knowledge; we show you how you can best deal with the AO2 requirement of the question. **This means that when you meet these sorts of question in your exam, you will know how to tackle them effectively in order to score high marks**.

For the last part of the questions (which is worth more marks) we also provide an **additional short commentary** alongside the students' answers, pointing out what is good, not so good and what is missing.

3 'Don't forget...' boxes

These boxes highlight some of the most important things to remember when answering questions on a particular topic. They also highlight some of the common mistakes that students make when answering exam questions in that area. When you're doing your last-minute revision you can quickly read through these boxes in all six chapters and make doubly sure you are ready to answer questions without making any easily avoidable mistakes.

4 'Key points to remember'

The 'Key points to remember' section of each chapter gives you a quick overview of the topic as a whole and presents the most important points that you will need to cover when revising that topic. Remember, however, that a book of this size can't hope to cover all the detailed psychological information that you need for your exam – that's what your textbook, class notes and assignments are for! Make sure you use these alongside this book.

5 Question to try, Answers and Examiner's comments

Each chapter ends with an exam question for you to try answering. The best way to do this is to try to answer it as if you were in an exam. Try to remember all that you've read earlier in the chapter and put it into practice here. It is particularly important to keep to the same times for each question that you would be allowed in the proper exam. It is best to find out now just what the time pressures are going to be like in your exam.

When you've written your answer, check it through and turn to the back of the book. There you'll find an answer to the question that you've just done. The answer is of a very good 'A' grade standard. **We've added our 'Examiner's comments' on it to show you exactly why it's such a good answer**.

Compare your answer with the answer given. If you feel yours isn't as good, you can use the one given and our comments on it to help you decide which aspects of your answer you could improve on. You may find, for example, that you can incorporate sections of the answer given into your own answer, and **you can use our comments to judge whether your own answer has covered the key issues**. Remember, though, that there is no such thing as a 'perfect answer'. If your answer and the 'model' answer differ merely in content, then yours may be every bit as good as the one given here, and would warrant just as many marks.

In the AQA–A exam, you will sit three exam papers or 'units'. Each of these corresponds to the material from a 'module'. You have to study all the material in these modules, although there will be a choice of questions in the exam. All of the three 'subsections' in each area (e.g. 'Stress as a bodily response', 'Sources of stress' and 'Stress management') will be represented across the two questions from which you make your choice. This doesn't mean that all three will be in each question, but it does mean that you can't afford to be selective in your revision. The advice given in the '**Choosing the best question**' part of each chapter will help you make the right decision when choosing which of the two questions to answer. There are also two questions in the Research Methods section, but you have to answer **both** of these.

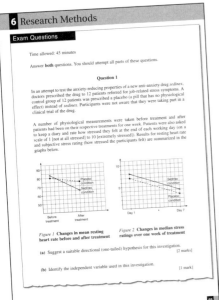

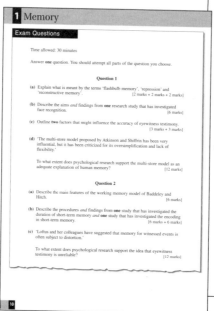

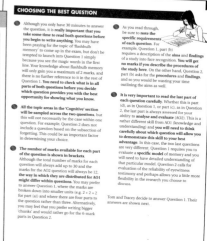

AO1, AO2 and AO3

AQA–A AS level questions assess **three types of skill**. These skills, known as 'Assessment Objectives', are as follows:

Knowledge and Understanding (AO1)

Analysis and Evaluation (AO2)

Designing, Conducting and Reporting (AO3)

AO3 questions are restricted to the Research Methods section, but AO1 and AO2 questions are present in all the other topics. Each question is worth 30 marks, with the AO1 parts of the question being worth 18 marks and the AO2 part of each question being worth 12 marks.

The first two (or three) parts of each question (except for Research Methods) are always AO1 and the last part always AO2. This is important because AO1 and AO2 questions require different types of answer. AO1 questions require more **descriptive responses**, whereas AO2 questions require more **evaluative responses**. The AO2 questions are always preceded by a short quotation or 'vignette' that drives the question that follows.

Examples of the types of questions

The following are examples of the types of questions that are used to assess AO1 and AO2. (This book contains many more such examples.) Remember that each mark is equivalent to approximately **one minute** of thinking and writing, so it is vital to use this time wisely, neither extending it nor skimping on it.

AO1 questions

What is meant by the terms conformity, minority influence, and obedience?

[2 + 2 + 2 marks]

Describe two differences between short-term (STM) and long-term (LTM) memory.

[3 + 3 marks]

Describe the aims and conclusions of one study of face recognition.　　[6 marks]

Describe the procedures and findings of one study of conformity.　　[6 marks]

Outline findings of research into the effects of day care on children's social development.

[6 marks]

Outline one explanation of attachment (e.g. Bowlby).　　[6 marks]

Outline two explanations of forgetting in short-term memory.　　[3 + 3 marks]

Give two criticisms of the levels of processing theory of memory.　　[3 + 3 marks]

AO2 questions

'Although psychologists believe eyewitness testimony to be the least trustworthy form of evidence for guilt, jurors appear to be more persuaded by this than by any other kind of evidence.'

To what extent has psychological research shown eyewitness testimony to be unreliable?

[12 marks]

'The role of ethical guidelines is to preserve the integrity and well-being of those who participate in research.'

Evaluate the use of ethical guidelines as a way of resolving ethical issues in psychological research.

[12 marks]

'What is considered "normal" or "abnormal" cannot be understood without also considering the cultural context of the behaviour being evaluated.'

Consider how attempts to define abnormality might be influenced by cultural differences.

[12 marks]

How marks are awarded

The following tables give an insight into how the marks are awarded for the most common of the AQA–A question types used in the AS level Psychology exam. These are **summaries** of the marking allocation tables used by examiners, but **they contain the same mark divisions and criteria**.

In the **AO1** questions, the emphasis is on the **amount of relevant material presented** (e.g. 'limited' or 'basic'), **the amount of detail given** (e.g. 'lacking detail') and **the accuracy of the material** (e.g. 'muddled').

In the **AO2** questions, the emphasis is on the **amount and level of the critical commentary** (e.g. 'superficial'), **its thoroughness** (e.g. 'reasonably thorough') and **how effectively it has been used** (e.g. 'highly effective').

AO1 2-mark questions

For example:

> What is meant by the terms conformity, minority influence and obedience?   [2 + 2 + 2 marks]

2 marks Accurate and detailed
1 mark Basic, lacking detail, muddled or flawed
0 marks Inappropriate or incorrect

AO1 3- and 6-mark questions

For example:

> Outline two explanations of forgetting in short-term memory.   [3 + 3 marks]
>
> Outline findings of research into the effects of day care on children's social development.   [6 marks]

3-mark questions	6-mark questions	Criteria
3	6-5	Accurate and detailed
2	4-3	Limited, generally accurate but less detailed
1	2-1	Basic, lacking in detail, muddled or flawed
0	0	Inaccurate or irrelevant

AO2 questions

As all AO2 questions are worth 12 marks, the following table applies to **all the questions** that you will encounter in the exam. The heading 'Commentary' applies to the specific AO2 requirement of the question (e.g. 'Evaluate' or 'To what extent?').

Marks	Commentary	Analysis	Use of material
12-11	Informed	Thorough	Highly effective
10-9	Informed	Reasonably thorough	Effective
8-7	Reasonable	Slightly limited	Effective
6-5	Reasonable	Limited	Reasonably effective
4-3	Superficial	Rudimentary	Minimal interpretation
2-1	Just discernible	Weak and muddled	Mainly irrelevant
0	Wholly irrelevant	Wholly irrelevant	Wholly irrelevant

Quality of Written Communication (QoWC)

The AQA–A AS Psychology exam also includes **an assessment of your written communication skills**. There are up to two marks awarded in each unit paper. That isn't a great deal, but it helps to know that they are there and how you can make sure you get them! The table below may help you in this:

2 marks	Accurate and clear expression of ideas, a broad range of specialist terms and only minor errors in grammar, punctuation and spelling.
1 mark	Reasonable expression of ideas, a reasonable range of specialist terms and few errors of grammar, punctuation and spelling.
0 marks	Poor expression of ideas, limited use of specialist terms and poor grammar, punctuation and spelling

Exam Tips

- **Read the questions carefully**, as marks are only available for the specific requirements of the question set. Miss those out and you lose marks; include something irrelevant and you've wasted valuable time.

- **Make a brief plan** before answering the question. This may be in your head or it may be on paper, but you must know where you are going and how long it will take you to get there. **Time management is absolutely vital**.

- Sometimes questions ask you to **outline** something. You need to practise doing this as the skill of précis is not as easy as it looks.

- **Be aware of the difference between AO1 and AO2 questions**. AO2 questions are not just an opportunity for more descriptive content. You must **engage with the question topic** in the required way.

- **Mind your language**. All exams now carry additional marks for **Quality of Written Communication** (QoWC). This is an assessment of your expression of ideas, use of specialist terms and your grammar, punctuation and spelling.

- **Use this book as it is intended**. The aim of this book is not to provide you with a set of 'model answers' but to give you skills and insights so you can use your own knowledge and critical skills more effectively in your exam.

Exam Questions

Time allowed: 30 minutes

Answer **one** question. You should attempt all parts of the question you choose.

Question 1

(a) Explain what is meant by the terms 'flashbulb memory', 'repression' and 'reconstructive memory'. [2 marks + 2 marks + 2 marks]

(b) Describe the aims *and* findings from **one** research study that has investigated face recognition. [6 marks]

(c) Outline **two** factors that might influence the accuracy of eyewitness testimony. [3 marks + 3 marks]

(d) 'The multi-store model proposed by Atkinson and Shiffrin has been very influential, but it has been criticized for its oversimplification and lack of flexibility.'

To what extent does psychological research support the multi-store model as an adequate explanation of human memory? [12 marks]

Question 2

(a) Describe the main features of the working memory model of Baddeley and Hitch. [6 marks]

(b) Describe the procedures *and* findings from **one** study that has investigated the duration of short-term memory *and* **one** study that has investigated the encoding in short-term memory. [6 marks + 6 marks]

(c) 'Loftus and her colleagues have suggested that memory for witnessed events is often subject to distortion.'

To what extent does psychological research support the idea that eyewitness testimony is unreliable? [12 marks]

CHOOSING THE BEST QUESTION

Although you only have 30 minutes to answer the question, it is **really important that you take some time to read both questions before you begin to write anything**. You may have been praying for the topic of 'flashbulb memory' to come up in the exam, but don't be tempted to launch into Question 1 simply because you see the magic words in the first line. Your knowledge about flashbulb memory will only gain you a maximum of 2 marks, and there is no further reference to it in the rest of Question 1. **You need to check what is in all parts of both questions before you decide which question provides you with the best opportunity for showing what you know.**

All the topic areas in the 'Cognitive' section will be sampled across the two questions, but this will not necessarily be the case within one question. For example, Question 2 does not include a question based on the subsection of forgetting. This could be an important factor in determining your choice.

The number of marks available for each part of the question is shown in brackets. Although the total number of marks for each question will always add up to 30 and the marks for the AO2 question will always be 12, **the way in which they are distributed for AO1 might differ within questions.** You may prefer to answer Question 1, where the marks are broken down into smaller units (e.g. 2 + 2 + 2 for part (a)) and where there are four parts to the question rather than three. Alternatively, you may feel that you prefer writing bigger 'chunks' and would rather go for the 6-mark parts in Question 2.

As you read through, be sure to **note the specific requirements of each question**. For example, Question 1, part (b) requires a description of the **aims** and **findings** of a study into face recognition. **You will get no marks if you describe the procedures of the study here**. On the other hand, Question 2, part (b) asks for the **procedures** and **findings**, and so you would be wasting your time outlining the aims as well.

It is very important to read the last part of each question carefully. Whether this is part (d), as in Question 1, or part (c), as in Question 2, the last part is always assessed for your ability to **analyse and evaluate** (AO2). This is a rather different skill from AO1 (knowledge and understanding) and **you will need to think carefully about which question will allow you to demonstrate this skill to your best advantage**. In this case, the two last questions are very different. Question 1 requires you to evaluate a **specific model** of memory and you will need to have detailed understanding of that particular model. Question 2 calls for evaluation of the reliability of eyewitness testimony and perhaps allows you a little more flexibility in the research you choose to discuss.

Tom and Tracey decide to answer Question 1. Their answers are shown next.

(a) Explain what is meant by the terms 'flashbulb memory', 'repression' and 'reconstructive memory'. [2 marks + 2 marks + 2 marks]

TOM'S ANSWER

Vivid memory for an event like Princess Diana dying — something sticks in your mind because it is important. Not remembering something because it is too horrible. Forgetting something.

TRACEY'S ANSWER

Flashbulb memory is when you remember something that is particularly important or unusual. It can be something that is in the newspapers like the death of Princess Diana or it can be something personal to you like your wedding day. You usually remember the details like where you were and who was with you and what the weather was like even after a long time. Repression is to do with Freud. It means pushing something away in your mind. Reconstructive memory means that you have something in your memory but it's not quite accurate — it's changed.

(b) Describe the aims *and* findings from **one** research study that has investigated face recognition. [6 marks]

TOM'S ANSWER

Young and Bruce said that you do not recognize people if they are in a different place — so, if you see your doctor at the swimming pool without his suit on and not in his surgery, you won't recognize him. They called this the 'Red Riding Hood effect'.

TRACEY'S ANSWER

Bahrick wanted to know if college lecturers would recognize their students' faces after they had stopped teaching them. He used photos of students that lecturers had taught several times a week for a ten-week course. He showed the photos to the lecturers but he mixed them up with photos of other students. He showed them a few days after the end of the course and then again after a year and after eight years. He found that teachers were good at picking out the students after a short delay and that they were still quite good after a year (about 50%). After 8 years, though, they were not very good at recognizing the students at all. *(5/6)*

(c) Outline **two** factors that might influence the accuracy of eyewitness testimony.

[3 marks + 3 marks]

TOM'S ANSWER

One thing that affects accuracy is misleading information. Loftus found that memory for events can be changed by false information given to people later on. For example, they will wrongly believe that they have seen a barn on a video clip if someone puts the idea into their heads by asking a misleading question. Another factor is something called the weapon focus. If you see someone carrying a gun, you are likely to look at that instead of the person.

(3/3)
(2/3)

TRACEY'S ANSWER

Misleading questions make a difference to how well witnesses remember things. They can be fooled by these questions into remembering things that were not there.

Another factor is the cognitive interview which makes people more accurate.

(2/3)
(1/3)

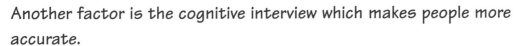

How to score full marks

Part (a)

 TOM'S ANSWER

Although Tom has given the explanations for the terms in the order they were set out in the question, **he does not make it explicitly clear which term is being explained. It would be better to state the term at the beginning of each explanation so that the examiner is left in no doubt**. You will notice that Tom has not written in proper sentences. As long as the sense is clear, this should not affect his marks for the question. However, **you need to remember that there are marks on each paper for quality of written communication (QoWC), and Tom could be penalized here if he does not write clearly and accurately**. Tom has conveyed an accurate and reasonably detailed explanation of 'flashbulb memory'. It has helped that he has provided a good example, e.g. the death of Princess Diana. **Appropriate examples can often be a useful way of clarifying your explanation**. His explanation of 'repression' is **limited and lacks detail**, but conveys the essence of what is meant by the term and so he gains 1 mark for this. To gain full marks, it would be useful to refer to the unconscious nature of repressed memories or, perhaps, to give an example of the kind of memory that might be repressed. **The last explanation, however, is far too vague** and tells us nothing about the specific nature of 'reconstructive memory', so Tom earns no marks for this.

TRACEY'S ANSWER

Tracey has been a bit more successful on this question. **She has given a detailed and accurate explanation of 'flashbulb memory'**. She, too, has provided good **examples**, and she has conveyed the important information that such memories are vivid, accurate and long-lasting, so earns 2/2. **She has been less clear in her explanation of 'repression', and this is why she has scored only 1 mark.** The term is certainly associated with Freud and involves suppressing information, but she has not explained why such memories are 'pushed away' (i.e., because they provoke anxiety). **Her third explanation shows some understanding of the term 'reconstructive memory', but it also lacks detail and scores only 1 mark. For full marks, she needs to explain that we do not store information passively, but, instead, weave it into our existing stores of knowledge and past experience (schemas).** When we later come to recall this information, it is often distorted.

Part (b)

TOM'S ANSWER

Sadly for Tom, he has misunderstood this question. **This highlights the importance of reading the questions carefully and making sure that you understand some of the basic terms.** Tom has accurately described a phenomenon (the Little Red Riding Hood effect) first identified by Young and Bruce. However, this is **not a study** – it is a factor affecting the accuracy of face recognition/eyewitness testimony (note that this could have been used effectively as an answer to part (c)). **Since no study has been described, Tom cannot be awarded any marks here.** There are several studies which Tom could have chosen, e.g. a study by Valentine and Bruce (1986), in which they investigated the effects of distinctiveness on face recognition; a study by Yarmey (1993) investigating the links between stereotyping and face recognition; or the study chosen by Tracey.

TRACEY'S ANSWER

Tracey has chosen an appropriate study and appears to know it reasonably well, although she has wasted some time in describing procedural detail when the question only requires **aims and findings. Note that she will not lose marks for including irrelevant material, but that she penalizes herself in terms of wasted time.** She has made a good attempt at describing the aims of the study (i.e., in her first sentence), although **it would have been a fuller answer if she had indicated certain key points,** i.e., Bahrick wanted to see if accurate recognition of familiar faces would become progressively worse over time without repeated exposure. Perhaps Tracey felt that she could only explain the findings if she had first described the procedure, but this is not necessary. She could have omitted all the procedural detail and simply included an extra sentence in her summary of findings, such as: 'Bahrick's results consisted of the number of student photos correctly identified by lecturers from a set of target and distractor photos'. **This would have conveyed succinctly as much of the procedure as was required to explain the findings.** Tracey's knowledge of the actual results is detailed and fairly accurate, although she could have given a fuller answer by quantifying the nature of the short delay (11 days) and by explaining that 'good' recall at this stage was still less than 100 per cent (i.e., 69 per cent). As it is, she earns 5/6.

Part (c)

TOM'S ANSWER

The first factor given by Tom is outlined well and deserves 3/3. **He has clearly identified a factor**, i.e., misleading information, **and elaborated on this by explaining that it occurs after the event**. He also makes it clear from his example that such information is likely to have an adverse effect on accuracy. He has chosen a perfectly appropriate second factor in 'the weapon focus', but he has not outlined this as clearly and so earns only 2/3. **He should have added that the anxiety provoked by the sight of a weapon distracts attention from other aspects of the attacker or of the scene and so reduces accuracy of recall for the whole event.**

TRACEY'S ANSWER

Tracey has also chosen to outline the influence of misleading information, **but has not given quite as much detail as Tom and so earns only 2/3.** She could have used an **example** to provide a fuller answer. She has chosen 'the cognitive interview' as her second factor and this could have formed the basis of a good answer, but she has not explained it well and scores only 1/3. It is perfectly acceptable to choose a factor that enhances rather than impairs accuracy (the question simply asks for factors that might **influence** accuracy), **but Tracey has not given any indication as to why the cognitive interview aids recall. For full marks, she needs to outline the procedures involved in the cognitive interview**, i.e., recreating the context, reporting every detail, recalling events in different orders and changing perspectives, **and to explain that these procedures seem to help witnesses to recall events more accurately.**

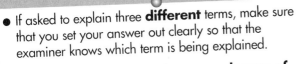

Don't forget ...

- If asked to explain three **different** terms, make sure that you set your answer out clearly so that the examiner knows which term is being explained.

- Explanations of terms **require some degree of detail**. You will not get marks for vague answers.

- **Make sure that you understand** what is meant by terms such as **'study'**. If you are asked to describe a study, you will gain no marks for describing a theory or an anecdote.

- **Read the questions carefully**. If you are asked to provide a description of the **aims and findings**, you will gain **no credit** for descriptions of the **procedures**.

- If you are asked to **outline** two factors that might influence, for example, eyewitness testimony, you must make sure that you demonstrate **how** the factors exert their influence. It is not enough simply to identify an appropriate factor.

Tom's answer to Question 1, part (d)

(d) 'The multi-store model proposed by Atkinson and Shiffrin has been very influential, but it has been criticized for its oversimplification and lack of flexibility.'

To what extent does psychological research support the multi-store model as an adequate explanation of human memory? [12 marks]

> **Tom is wasting time here – this material is *descriptive* rather than *evaluative* and will *not* gain any credit. There is no time to write a broad introduction to the topic of memory.**

Memory is very important to humans. Without it, they would not be able to remember anything about themselves or how to do anything. A man called Clive Wearing lost his memory after an illness and it was like being in a living hell. Lots of psychologists have studied memory. The first people to come up with a theory were Atkinson and Shiffrin. They called it the multi-store model but it is also called the modal model. It has three parts which are sensory memory, short-term memory and long-term memory.

> **This could be a good AO2 point supporting the Atkinson and Shiffrin (A & S) idea that there is a different store for each sensory modality. Unfortunately, Tom does not make this point *explicit*.**

Sensory memory can only hold things for a very brief time. Sperling showed that it lasts for about 1/2 a second if you look at letters, but someone else found that it lasts for 2 seconds if you hear sounds.

> **This is simply a description of Miller's findings. How does this relate to the A & S model?**

Short-term memory holds about 7 items. This was found out by Miller, but he said that we could hold more if we put them in chunks.

> **At last! Tom is beginning to introduce material to *support* the multi-store theory.**
> **Another evaluative point. Tom has introduced a different theory (levels of processing) to *criticize* the multi-store model.**

Atkinson and Shiffrin say that we have to repeat things over and over if we want to keep them in short-term memory. If we repeat them enough, they will go into long-term memory but if we cannot repeat them, they are lost. Brown and Peterson gave people nonsense words to remember but did not let them repeat them. They forgot them very quickly which shows that repeating is important. Craik and Lockhart criticized this. They said that repeating on its own is not enough — you need to process the words and the deeper you process them, the more likely you are to remember them.

> **Amnesia studies can be useful to evaluate the A & S model, but Tom does not explain *how* and he does not demonstrate a good understanding of the amnesia research.**

People with amnesia support the multi-store model. Clive Wearing can remember things at this moment (short-term memory) but he can't remember the past (long-term memory). HM who had an operation for epilepsy was the same. KF who had a motorbike accident was different, though. He had a bad short-term memory but his long-term memory seemed all right. This is difficult for Atkinson and Shiffrin to explain.

4/12

Tracey's answer to Question 1, part (d)

(d) 'The multi-store model proposed by Atkinson and Shiffrin has been very influential, but it has been criticized for its oversimplification and lack of flexibility.'

To what extent does psychological research support the multi-store model as an adequate explanation of human memory? [12 marks]

> **If you feel you have the time, it is worth setting out *briefly* the central assumptions of the model, as Tracey does here.**
> **Tracey is using the Sperling material to *support* the model.**
> **Evaluative point, although it is not *explicitly* linked to the A & S model.**

Atkinson and Shiffrin put forward the multi-store model which is a structural model of memory. They thought that memory was divided up into 3 separate stores called sensory, short-term and long-term memory. There is a lot of support for this idea. Sperling investigated sensory memory and found that it held visual information for only about 50 milliseconds. If it is not passed on to STM in that time, it will be lost. Treisman, while researching attention, found that sensory memory for auditory information lasts a bit longer – approx. 2 seconds. This seems to suggest that sensory memory is different for different senses.

> **This is a good point. It shows how the evidence that is cited is *relevant*, i.e., there is empirical support for the idea of different structures within memory.**

STM and LTM seem to work differently in several ways. For example, Miller showed that STM can only hold 7 + or −2 items, but it seems that LTM can hold as much as you want. The two stores also use different coding methods according to Baddeley. STM prefers acoustic coding and LTM prefers semantic coding. Finally, STM only lasts for a few seconds and LTM lasts for ever. These differences show that the two stores must be separate.

> **Another good point. Tracey contrasts the unitary store in the A & S model with the more complex nature of the working memory model.**

Not everyone agrees with this. Baddeley thinks the model is too simple. He put forward the idea of working memory which allows STM to do different tasks. Atkinson and Shiffrin said STM was just a storehouse.

> **Now she contrasts the multi-store model with the levels of processing model, although this point is not well developed.**

Atkinson and Shiffrin thought that we transfer information into LTM by rehearsing it. Other psychologists think that deep processing is necessary to transfer information.

> **Is Tracey running out of time? She should not start asking questions. She is hinting at an important point here, but she does not *develop* it. The appraisal of the model as 'good' and 'fair' is a bit vague and not supported by evidence. The reference to the amnesia research is relevant, but poorly explained.**

Why is it that we remember some things better than others? The multi-store model does not explain this. I think it has been a very good model and it is very fair but there is a lot it does not explain like some patients with amnesia who are able to use LTM without going through STM.

7/12

Avoid irrelevant material

You will have approximately 12 minutes to write this part of the answer, so you do not have time to waste. It is important to engage with the question from the beginning. Do not waste time with a lengthy introductory paragraph that does little to address the question (as Tom did). In this example, it is not necessary to explain what is meant by memory, nor to give a history of research. **You need to engage from the outset with the adequacy of the multi-store model**.

Use specialist vocabulary

You need to write grammatically and in complete sentences, but Tom has wasted time in writing out the terms 'short-term memory' and 'long-term memory' several times. **It is perfectly acceptable to use the abbreviations STM and LTM**. It is important in this type of question to be able to **express ideas succinctly**. It often helps if you are able to use **specialist terms** and can remember the names of **key researchers**, as this can condense the number of words required. For example, **Tom could have dealt with sensory memory more economically and made an evaluative point at the same time** by saying: 'According to Atkinson and Shiffrin, there is a store for each of the *sensory modalities*. This was confirmed by *Sperling*, who investigated the *iconic store*, and *Treisman*, who found evidence for an *echoic store*. One way that shows that they operate independently is that they have different *durations*.' (Specialist terms and names shown in italics.)

Make your evaluative points clear

Tom has also made the mistake of **describing** facts or findings about the multi-store model **without drawing appropriate conclusions**. For example, **his short paragraph about the capacity of STM provides neither support nor criticism of the multi-store model** and so can gain no marks. Tracey deals with this better by introducing her paragraph with the sentence: 'STM and LTM seem to work differently in several ways.' In this way, she signals that she is **evaluating** a key concept in the multi-store model, i.e., that STM and LTM are separate and operate differently.

Consider strengths and weaknesses: strengths

In this type of question, you need to think about the strengths and weaknesses of the model in order to demonstrate its adequacy as an explanation. One positive aspect is that it was one of the first testable models of memory and it provided a basic framework that could be expanded by later researchers. For example, the working memory model as an extension of the concept of STM (**Baddeley and Hitch**) and the idea of semantic/episodic/procedural memory (**Tulving**) as a way of understanding LTM. There is support for the model in terms of its fundamental distinction between STM and LTM. Evidence that could be cited here is **Murdock's** free recall studies, and also any studies that show a distinction between the methods of operation of STM and LTM, e.g. **Miller's** research into the capacity of STM, or **Baddeley's** studies into the relative encoding strategies of the two stores. **Case studies of people with amnesia induced by brain damage could be used effectively to support the distinction between STM and LTM**. The role of rehearsal, which is central to the **Atkinson and Shiffrin** model, could be supported by research based on the **Brown–Peterson** technique and could be contrasted with the levels of processing approach, which stressed the nature rather than the amount of rehearsal.

Consider strengths and weaknesses: weaknesses

You have been asked in this question to assess the **extent** to which psychological research supports the multi-store model, but **this does not mean that you must only focus on evidence that is in favour of the model. By assessing the extent, you also need to consider the counter-evidence.** Weaknesses of the model include the fact that it is **too simple** – Atkinson and Shiffrin seem to make the assumption that all material is remembered in the same way and **they do not take into account the fact that certain things are easier to recall** (e.g. film stars' names rather than psychology researchers' names!). **Other theories, such as levels of processing, can explain this better.** There is also **evidence** to suggest that the **flow of information through the system is not always one way,** as Atkinson and Shiffrin suggested. For example, visually presented letters registering on sensory memory are translated into an acoustic code for access to STM – this can only happen if the individual is first able to obtain information about letter shapes and sounds from LTM. **The idea that LTM can only be accessed through STM has also been undermined by the case study of KF,** whose STM capacity was grossly impaired but who seemed able to transfer new items into LTM. **The role of the STM as a simple, unitary storage unit has been questioned by Baddeley and Hitch,** who have produced evidence to support the idea of a multi-component STM. The emphasis on structural components in the multi-store model has been criticized by **Craik and Lockhart,** who have shown that processes might be more important than structures.

Don't forget ...

- The **last part** of all AS questions (except for 'Research Methods') is **worth 12 marks**, so allow yourself adequate time (approximately 12 minutes) to answer it in sufficient depth.

- This last part of the question will be assessing your ability to **analyse and evaluate** theories, concepts, studies and methods and to **communicate** your knowledge and understanding of psychology **in a clear and effective manner** (AO2 or Assessment Objective 2). **You will not gain marks here by simply describing theories or research.**

- Remember that you need to **consider both sides of the argument** when you are asked to assess the extent to which a theory/model is supported.

- **Two marks are allocated for the quality of written communication** shown in a paper. It is worthwhile trying to write clearly and accurately, using specialist terms correctly.

Human memory

Human memory refers to the **mental processes** we use in order to acquire, store, retrieve and use our knowledge about the world.

Short-term memory and long-term memory

Short-term memory (STM) is a system for storing information for brief periods of time. For some researchers (e.g. **Atkinson and Shiffrin**), it is seen as a temporary storage box for information. For others (e.g. **Baddeley and Hitch**), it is seen as a more complex system consisting of different working components. It is generally accepted that the capacity of STM is limited, although whether it is limited by the number of items it can hold (e.g. **Miller**) or by time restraints (e.g. Baddeley and Hitch) is a matter for discussion. **Long-term memory (LTM)**, in contrast, is thought to have an infinite capacity and is able to store a huge range of information over long periods of time. There are several theories that have been proposed which attempt to explain human memory processes. The **multi-store model** mainly associated with Atkinson and Shiffrin focuses on the **structural aspects of memory** and distinguishes between sensory, short-term and long-term memory. These structures are thought to differ from one another in terms of capacity, duration and encoding. Baddeley and Hitch focused on the STM, but thought that it was a much more complex system than Atkinson and Shiffrin. Their **working memory model** comprises a set of slave-systems under the control of a central executive. A rather different model was proposed by **Craik and Lockhart**, who believed that the crucial factor in laying down new memories is the amount and depth of processing they receive. For this reason, their model is called the **levels of processing theory**.

Forgetting

We cannot remember everything that enters the memory system and psychologists have been interested in investigating some of the reasons why we forget. Forgetting seems to occur rather differently in the two main stores. In **STM**, the main mechanisms for forgetting are **decay** and **displacement**, whereas in **LTM**, it seems that **retrieval failure** and **interference** are the most likely reasons why we forget. Sometimes our ability to remember can be influenced by our emotional state. **Flashbulb memories** are vivid, accurate and long-lasting memories for events which have particular significance for us. In this case, **emotional involvement** appears to improve our recall. **Freud**, however, believed that **strong emotions could sometimes interfere with accurate recall**. He described **repression** as an unconscious process whereby a distressing memory or impulse is excluded from conscious awareness.

Critical issue: Eyewitness testimony

One particular area of interest for memory researchers is the field of eyewitness testimony. Although people are sometimes able to recall events with high degrees of accuracy, **eyewitness testimony can be unreliable**. One possible reason is that memories are **distorted or reconstructed**. **Bartlett** first introduced the idea of **reconstructive memory**, whereby we store memories in terms of our past knowledge and experience (schemas). A more recent researcher in this field is **Elizabeth Loftus**, who has been particularly concerned with the effects of **misleading information** provided after the event. One particular aspect of eyewitness testimony is the **ability to recognize faces**. We are quite skilled at recognizing faces that are familiar to us and faces that are particularly distinctive. Perhaps not surprisingly, we are less competent at recognizing faces seen only once or from only one angle.

Question for you to try

Examiner's hints

● In part (a), you are **only** required to write about the working memory model. **Do not** waste time by writing a general introduction about other models of memory.

● Take care that you choose studies in part (b) where you are able to describe **both** the proceedures **and** the findings.

● Remember, too, that you have to describe **two** studies in part (b) – these descriptions will be assessed **independently** (i.e., 6 marks for each), so make sure that you spend **about the same time on each study**.

● In part (c) you **do not have to refer directly to the quotation** and you do not have to restrict your answer to research by Loftus.

● Remember that in part (c) you need to show your skills in **analysing and evaluating** eyewitness testimony research.

Q2

(a) Describe the main features of the working memory model of Baddeley and Hitch. [6 marks]

(b) Describe the procedures *and* findings from **one** study that has investigated the duration of short-term memory *and* **one** study that has investigated the encoding in short-term memory. [6 marks + 6 marks]

(c) 'Loftus and her colleagues have suggested that memory for witnessed events is often subject to distortion.'

To what extent does psychological research support the idea that eyewitness testimony is unreliable? [12 marks]

Answers are given on pp. 82–83.

Time allowed: 30 minutes

Answer **one** question. You should attempt all parts of the question you choose.

Question 1

(a) Outline **two** features of early attachment.   [3 marks + 3 marks]

(b) Describe **one** explanation of attachment.   [6 marks]

(c) Describe the procedures *and* findings from **one** study of attachment.   [6 marks]

(d) 'Securely attached infants may have an advantage over insecurely attached infants in terms of their future development.'

   To what extent has it been shown that the nature of children's early attachments influence their later development?   [12 marks]

Question 2

(a) Explain what is meant by the following terms: 'maternal deprivation'; 'privation'; 'secure attachment'.   [2 marks + 2 marks + 2 marks]

(b) Describe the findings *and* conclusions from **one** study investigating the short-term effects of separation of children from their primary caregiver, and from **one** study of the long-term effects of deprivation *or* privation.   [6 marks + 6 marks]

(c) 'In many industrialized countries it is typical for infants as well as school-aged children to spend significant periods of time being cared for by someone other than a parent.'

   Consider the possible benefits and/or disadvantages of day care for children's social and/or cognitive development.   [12 marks]

CHOOSING THE BEST QUESTION

• **Be sure to read both questions carefully before you start writing**. In this way you will select the question that will enable you to score the highest marks. **Do a rough calculation to work out how many marks in each question you think you can achieve**. Don't just make up your mind on the basis of the first couple of parts in each question. Which of the questions on page 1 would you choose?

• Although all topic areas in 'Attachments in Development' will be sampled over the two questions, this will not necessarily occur within any one question. **Take care not to rush into answering a question just because the first couple of parts are about an area you particularly enjoyed**. Later parts may ask you about another area altogether. Of course, sometimes a question will deal with only one or two topics.

• Whether or not you have preferences for individual topics, you will still need to **read each part of the two questions carefully and note their specific requirements**. If you prefer to give fairly short answers, then Question 2 may be more attractive to you since part (a) is divided into three sections rather than two, as in Question 1, part (a). Note, however, that you are asked for information about two studies of separation effects in Question 2. If you know about only one study, you could sacrifice 6 marks. **Consider also whether you can separate out findings from conclusions**.

Maybe you would prefer Question 1, where knowledge about the **procedures and findings** of **only one** study is required (in part (c)). If you are more confident about describing an **explanation** of attachment, then Question 1 may be a better option for you since 6 marks are allocated to this in part (b).

• **It is important to look at the last part of each question before choosing which to answer**. In Question 1 the focus of part (d) is the influence of early attachments on later development. In Question 2, the last part asks you to consider the 'critical' issue of day care and how it might affect social and/or cognitive development. **Remember that this last part of the question (worth 12 marks) always asks you to analyse and evaluate psychological material** and **to communicate your understanding clearly and effectively** (AO2 skills). Consider which of the two questions gives you the better chance to do this. Although the last part of a question is worth more than any other single part, the other parts together are worth 18 marks and test AO1 skills (knowledge and understanding). Therefore, **choose the question that gives you the chance to score the highest mark overall.**

Martin and Mary decide to answer Question 1. Their answers are shown next.

(a) Outline **two** features of early attachment. [3 marks + 3 marks]

MARTIN'S ANSWER

One feature of early attachment is that at 3 months children prefer familiar people.

Another feature is that as babies get older they form more than one attachment.

MARY'S ANSWER

When babies are about 7 or 8 months old they become attached to one person, usually the mother.

(b) Describe **one** explanation of attachment. [6 marks]

MARTIN'S ANSWER

Bowlby's theory of attachment is based on the theory of evolution. Babies become attached to their mother by instinct because this keeps them safe from danger and teaches them how to make relationships later in life. If an infant does not form an attachment they may have trouble with relationships later on. He said that babies become attached to only one person. Other people have criticized Bowlby's explanation. They say that babies can be attached to lots of people and that parents teach their children to love them.

MARY'S ANSWER

Behaviourists claim that conditioning causes attachment. If you are rewarded for doing something you are more likely to do it again. Babies like the mother best because she provides food.

(c) Describe the procedures *and* findings from **one** study of attachment. [6 marks]

MARTIN'S ANSWER

Klaus and Kennell carried out a study in a hospital to find out if there is a period just after a baby is born when the mother and baby will form attachments easily. Some babies spent very little time with their mothers immediately after the birth. Others had longer skin-to-skin contact time. They found that the mothers and babies who had extra skin-to-skin time were better attached later on.

(3/6)

MARY'S ANSWER

Harlow studied infant monkeys and showed that food is not the most important thing in developing attachments. He separated baby monkeys from their mothers to keep them free from germs so that they could be used in other studies. They began to act strangely and became bad parents. When the infants were scared (e.g. by a toy drummer) they ran to a cloth-covered model even though the wire model provided food. Therefore, food is not the most important thing.

(3/6)

How to score full marks

Part (a)

 Both Martin and Mary selected phases of attachment (based on Schaffer and Emerson's work) as features to outline. This is fine, but **both answers needed more detail**.

MARTIN'S ANSWER

Martin's answer earns only 1/3 for each of the features he outlines. **For full marks the answer needed to be both accurate and detailed**. For example, you could make the point that before infants form clear-cut attachments they begin to show a preference for familiar people, smiling at them more but still allowing strangers to handle and comfort them. The second feature Martin deals with also **needs more detail** for full marks. This could be given by referring to the way that once infants have formed a main attachment they will begin to develop other attachments, e.g. to grandparents or close family friends, thus establishing strong emotional ties to people other than the primary caregiver.

MARY'S ANSWER

Mary's answer deals with the phase of clear-cut (specific) attachment. The main characteristics of this phase are the fear of stranger response, when the infant shows anxiety (e.g. by crying) if a stranger tries to make contact with it, and becoming upset if the attachment object leaves. **With this extra detail you would gain full marks**. Unfortunately, **Mary deals with only one feature** and so gets 0/3 for the second feature required.

Part (b)

There are several explanations for attachment that you could use (e.g. learning theory, social learning theory, psychodynamic theory, Bowlby's theory) to answer the question.

MARTIN'S ANSWER

Martin chooses Bowlby's theory but his answer lacks detail, although it is generally accurate. Therefore he gains only 3/6. Note, however, that Bowlby did not claim that infants become attached to only one person, but rather that they have an innate tendency to form a strong, qualitatively different bond (attachment) with one individual, usually the mother. This is called his monotropy hypothesis. **For full marks you should describe the main features of Bowlby's explanation**: attachment as adaptive (i.e., it increases the infant's chances of survival and reproduction); the role of social releasers (such as crying) that produce a care-giving reaction from another person; the sensitive period for its development; proximity seeking by child; use of parent as safe base for exploration; and how the first attachment provides a template for future relationships. **Note that Martin gains no marks for giving criticisms of Bowlby's theory**, because the question asks for a **description** of one explanation, **not** for an evaluation.

MARY'S ANSWER

Mary's description of conditioning as an explanation of attachment is **basic and lacks detail**. Therefore, the answer earns only 2/6. **Ensure that you have a good grasp of the explanation you choose. For full marks you need to show clearly how behaviourists have explained attachment in terms of classical and operant conditioning**. For instance, the way a mother becomes associated with the pleasure an infant feels when it is fed is an example of classical conditioning. According to operant conditioning principles, rewarded behaviours are repeated. Instinctively, a baby is 'driven' to seek food when hungry. After feeding, the hunger 'drive' is reduced and this is rewarding. Therefore, when the baby is hungry again it repeats the behaviour (e.g. crying) that leads to the drive reduction. Since the mother provides the food (a primary reinforcer) to reduce the hunger drive, she becomes a secondary reinforcer (by the process of classical conditioning) and the infant strives to stay close to her. Thereby, the infant becomes attached.

Part (c)

There are many studies that it would be appropriate to describe in this answer. In addition to those chosen by Martin and Mary, you could describe, for example, studies of secure and insecure attachments using the **Strange Situation**, or **Schaffer and Emerson's study** of developing attachment in Glasgow infants, or any of the studies investigating how early attachments affect later development.

MARTIN'S ANSWER

Martin's answer begins by describing the aims of the **Klaus and Kennell** study. **This earns no marks as the question asks for procedures and findings**. This experiment focused on mothers' bonding with their infants rather than babies' attaching to their mothers, but since bonding can be taken as an example of attachment, it is appropriate to use it here. **The description of the procedures Martin gives is generally accurate but lacks detail and his description of the findings is very basic**. Therefore the answer gains only 3/6. The kind of detail needed to earn full marks includes such things as how long the extra contact was (six hours over a three-day period), how the findings were collected (by observation and interview), and when (at one month and one year on). Finally, **more detail about the findings themselves is required**, e.g. the mothers in the 'extended contact' condition showed more soothing behaviours when their infants were upset, stayed closer to them and made more face-to-face contact.

MARY'S ANSWER

Mary chooses to describe the famous **Harlow** study of infant monkeys. This is appropriate but her answer, though generally accurate, is **repetitive and lacking in detail** and so gains only 3/6. **For full marks, you need to be more precise and systematic about the procedures**. For example, you could give the age of the infants when separated from their real mothers, appearance of the substitute mothers, which one provided the milk, etc. For details of findings you could mention which substitute mother the infant monkeys preferred sitting on, how they reacted to frightening events, and the long-term effects on the monkeys' adult behaviour.

Don't forget ...

- If you are asked to outline or describe **more than one** feature or explanation, be sure to do so. Try to do each in appropriate detail, as each will be marked independently.

- If asked to describe **one** explanation, write about only one!

- Do not spend time giving **evaluations** if you are asked only to **describe**.

- When choosing a study to describe, try to select one about which you know enough of the **right sort of detail**.

- **When asked for a description, provide some detail**. A definition or short sentence is not enough. However, remember that you have only got three minutes approximately for a 3-mark answer, and six minutes for a 6-mark answer.

- **Watch out for plurals** in a question. If you are asked for finding**s**, this means more than one!

Martin's answer to Question 1, part (d)

(d) 'Securely attached infants may have an advantage over insecurely attached infants in terms of their future development.'

To what extent has it been shown that the nature of children's early attachments influence their later development? [12 marks]

> **Martin makes reasonable claims, but these need to be *supported by evidence*. Reference to studies by Hazan and Shaver and by Quinton et al. would have been appropriate here.**

It has been shown that securely attached infants turn into more confident and loving adults. They find it easier to form relationships and to be good parents themselves. This is what Bowlby said would happen and he was right.

> **This is a sweeping statement and *no evidence* is given to support it.**

If babies do not love their parents they do not know how to love their own children when the time comes for them to be parents.

> **Martin *does not relate this statement to the* question set.**

If you can form good relationships in life you will be happier and probably do better in school as you get on better with people.

> **Needs to be much *more evaluative* about *how* this study was conducted. Why is a control group important?**

Bowlby showed that some delinquent boys had been separated from their parents early in life and so probably did not form attachments. But there was no control group in this study.

> **A weak attempt at evaluation. The last sentence earns no marks as it neither demonstrates any psychological knowledge nor addresses the question set.**
>
> **Overall, Martin's answer is superficial and provides only a *rudimentary analysis* of whether or not early attachments influence later development.**

Some children (e.g. Czech twin boys abused by their parents) who have bad experiences early in life still do quite well later on. The world would be a better place though if only children formed good attachments when they were babies.

4/12

Mary's answer to Question 1, part (d)

(d) 'Securely attached infants may have an advantage over insecurely attached infants in terms of their future development.'

To what extent has it been shown that the nature of children's early attachments influence their later development? [12 marks]

Mary seems to be trying to prepare the way for a balanced assessment of the influence of early attachments on later development. She could have done this in one sentence. As it is, she is using time to do little more than rephrase the question.

A promising paragraph *giving relevant supporting evidence* for one point of view.

However, *too much detail about the procedure* given and *no evaluation* of this or the other studies given.

What a pity that Mary does not make this relevant to the question set.

Needs a concluding comment to readdress the question. Mary's opening paragraph led us to expect that both sides of the argument would be explored, but in the end only one point of view was given. Mary provides only a *limited analysis* of whether early attachments influence later development.

Some psychologists believe that the way we develop later in life can be affected by whether or not we were attached to our parents when we were babies. Other psychologists are less sure there is a direct causal link between early attachment and later development.

Many studies such as that by Grossman have shown that securely attached infants are more likely to have friends and be sociable than infants who were insecurely attached. A study by Hazan and Shaver also showed that people who were securely attached as babies had happy relationships when they were adults. A 'love quiz' was printed in a local paper and was answered by over 600 adults. It revealed the person's type of attachment in infancy and their romantic style as adults. Those who had been insecurely attached were more likely to be jealous or to think that they did not need love.

The Strange situation is used to assess if a baby is securely attached, but this technique might not be appropriate to use with babies from all cultures.

5/12

How to score full marks for part (d)

Answer the question set

With 12 marks to earn in a short period, it is important not to waste time. **Give only the information that is asked for**. Remember to **link all your points clearly to the question**. Always remember that this is the **AO2** part of the question (see pages 6–9), so structure your answer accordingly and **engage from the start with the question set**.

Evaluation skills

Your task is to arrive at an informed judgement as to whether or not early attachments influence later development, and you are primarily required to **show your skills of evaluation** here. There is no need to give procedural details of studies.

Validity of the Strange Situation

You could begin by briefly considering the **validity** of the Strange Situation as a technique for establishing the nature of an infant's attachment (see cross-cultural studies). If there is uncertainty about the means by which we assess the security of attachment, this throws into question the validity of any causal relationship existing between it and later development.

Correlation does not equal causation

Further to this point, you could challenge the idea that any link shown between infant attachments and later development is necessarily a **causal** one. Correlation does not equal causation. Consider also the view proposed by some psychologists that the nature of our adult intimate relationships is not dictated **solely** by our first attachment experience but is the **result of many factors interacting**. These factors include general expectations held in our society about how we should express ourselves in relationships, along with our own past experiences and those of our partner.

Evaluate the research

You can also tackle this question by examining **relevant empirical studies**. Consider, for example, which findings lend support to the view that there is some continuity between early attachments and later development. The studies of **Grossman and Grossman** (1991) found that children who had been securely attached to their mothers had more friends later in childhood. **Quinton et al.** (1988) found that women who had been reared in institutions and denied the opportunity to form close attachments made poor parents later. **Hazan and Shaver's study** (mentioned in Mary's answer) also supports the notion of a link between early attachment and the nature of later close relationships. It is important to **evaluate** these studies in terms of the **methods** they used and their **ecological validity**. A common criticism of research into adult relationships is that **demand characteristics arise**, where respondents tend to make generalizations about the nature of their relationships. Other research shows that people may be secure in some of their relationships but insecure in others.

Both sides of the debate

It is not essential that you give equal weight to the arguments or studies opposing the direct link between early attachments and later development. By **evaluating the studies** in support of the link (cited in the previous paragraph), you could achieve full marks. However, if you wish to give both sides of the argument (as Mary suggested she was going to do in her first paragraph), you could evaluate, for example, the temperament hypothesis, which proposes that our relationships in infancy and adulthood are best explained in terms of our innate temperament.

- The **last part** of all AS questions (except for 'Research Methods') is **worth 12 marks**, so allow yourself adequate time (approximately 12 minutes) to answer it in sufficient depth.

- This last part of the question will be assessing your ability to **analyse and evaluate** theories, concepts, studies and methods and to **communicate** your knowledge and understanding of psychology **in a clear and effective manner** (AO2 or Assessment Objective 2).

- **Two marks are allocated for the quality of written communication** shown in a paper. It is worthwhile trying to write clearly and accurately, using specialist terms correctly.

Key points to remember

Attachments in development

Attachment is a **strong, reciprocal, emotional tie that develops over time between an infant and a primary caregiver**. Its development depends upon the **interaction** of the two people. Infants are probably born with an innate tendency to develop an attachment.

Development and variety of attachments

Schaffer and Emerson proposed four phases in the **development of attachment**: pre-attachment, attachment-in-the-making, clear-cut attachment and multiple attachments. Some researchers have questioned the ages at which these stages occur. One of the most investigated **individual differences** in attachment concerns security/insecurity. **Ainsworth** studied the security of attachments using the **Strange Situation** and found that most infants were securely attached, while about 15 per cent were described as insecure avoidant and another 15 per cent as insecure ambivalent. An infant's **type of attachment** is thought to depend upon the **warmth and responsiveness of the caregiver** and to some extent upon the **innate temperament** of the infant. Attachments vary **across cultures**, although research seems to indicate that secure attachments are important in many cultures. The use of the Strange Situation across cultures and subcultures to assess the security of attachment has been criticized. Different **explanations of attachment** have been proposed. These include learning theory, psychodynamic theory and Bowlby's theory of attachment as an adaptive process.

Critical issue: Day care

Day care is the term used to describe the **care given to pre-school children by people other than a parent**. On the whole, research findings support the claim that day care causes no harm to development, and some children seem to benefit possibly because the day care compensates for the lack of opportunities at home.

Attachments to parents do not seem to be affected by day care. The **quality** of day care is important and can be improved by providing adequate resources, keeping low staff turnover, having low child–staff ratios, and training staff to be responsive to children's needs.

Deprivation and privation

Deprivation is the **loss** of something. In this context, it refers to a situation where a child is deprived of the love of its primary attachment figure. **Privation** is the **lack** of something. In this case, it refers to a situation where no attachment has ever been formed. Unless children are adequately prepared, the **short-term effects** of deprivation/separation may include **protest**, **despair** and **detachment**. If the separation is extended over a lengthy period, then the child may become **depressed**. Past experiences and the security of a child's attachment affect the way it responds to separation. According to **Bowlby's maternal deprivation hypothesis**, children who are unable to develop a continuous relationship with a mother figure are likely to experience difficulty with later relationships. **Critics of Bowlby** argue that children who are unable to form such an attachment with a mother figure are likely also to suffer other deprivations. **Rutter** also points out that even if there is an association between lack of attachment and later problems with relationships, this does **not** mean there is a cause-and-effect link. Family discord may have caused the separation and the subsequent problems. **Longitudinal studies** of children in institutions and **individual case studies** suggest that **recovery from privation is possible when good-quality emotional care is provided at a young enough age**.

Question for you to try

Examiner's hints
- Explain each of the three terms in part (a) **separately**. Each is marked independently.
- Concentrate on **findings and conclusions** for the two studies required in (b). Do not waste time on other aspects of these studies.
- In part (c) you **do not have to refer directly to the quotation**.
- Remember that in part (c) you need to show your **skills in analysing and evaluating** the possible benefits and/or disadvantages of day care for social and/or cognitive development.

(a) Explain what is meant by the following terms: 'maternal deprivation'; 'privation'; 'secure attachment'.

[2 marks + 2 marks + 2 marks]

(b) Describe the findings *and* conclusions from **one** study investigating the short-term effects of separation of children from their primary caregiver, and from **one** study of the long-term effects of deprivation or privation. [6 marks + 6 marks]

(c) 'In many industrialized countries it is typical for infants as well as school-aged children to spend significant periods of time being cared for by someone other than a parent.'

Consider the possible benefits and/or disadvantages of day care for children's social and/or cognitive development. [12 marks]

Answers are given on pp. 84–85.

Exam Questions

Time allowed: 30 minutes

Answer **one** question. You should attempt all parts of the question you choose.

Question 1

(a) What is meant by the terms 'stressor', 'stress inoculation' and 'hardiness'?

[2 marks + 2 marks + 2 marks]

(b) Describe **one** physical approach to stress management. [6 marks]

(c) Give **two** criticisms of the approach you have described in (b).

[3 marks + 3 marks]

(d) 'Women may live longer than men simply because they react differently to stress.'

To what extent are the effects of stress modified by gender differences?

[12 marks]

Question 2

(a) Outline **two** ways in which the body responds to stress. [3 marks + 3 marks]

(b) Outline research into the effects of stress on the immune system. [6 marks]

(c) Describe the procedures and conclusions of **one** research study that has investigated the role of the workplace as a source of stress. [6 marks]

(d) 'Somehow, when you feel in control of events around you, you don't feel quite as stressed.'

Evaluate the role of 'control' in the experience of stress. [12 marks]

Be sure to read both questions carefully before you start writing. In this way you will select the question that will enable you to score the highest marks. Do a rough calculation to work out how many marks in each question you think you can achieve. Don't just make up your mind on the basis of the first couple of parts in each question. Which of the questions on page 1 would you choose?

Although all topic areas in physiological psychology (i.e., 'Stress as a bodily response', 'Sources of stress' and 'Stress management') will be sampled over the two questions, this will not necessarily occur within any one question. Take care not to rush into answering a question just because you feel you can manage the first part or first couple of parts. It is easy, in the stress of an examination, to misread or misinterpret the exact requirements of a question. A couple of quiet minutes reading and thinking about which question you might choose will pay dividends later (i.e., you won't get halfway into a question and then realize you can't answer the latter parts).

You may have a preference for one topic rather than another (for example, 'Sources of stress' rather than 'Stress as a bodily response'). This does not mean that the question that contains this topic is overall the most profitable in terms of the total number of marks that you might achieve. Sometimes you have to forgo a favourite topic because the other parts of the question are not ones that you feel you can answer well. You will still need to read each part of the two questions carefully and note their specific requirements in order to make this decision. In Question 2, for example, part (c) asks you to describe the procedures and conclusions from one study that has investigated the role of the workplace as a source of stress. If you know nothing about the procedures of a study in this area or can't work out the conclusions, then this is clearly not the question for you!

It is very important to look at the last part of each question before choosing which to answer. The final part of each question is the AO2 part of that question, therefore you are being asked to do more than simply describe material that is relevant to the area. You are being asked to engage with the material in a specific way. In Question 1, you are asked 'to what extent…', which requires you to weigh up the evidence that the effects of stress really are modified by gender differences. You need to have a good overview of research or arguments around this area, and also be able to deal with these in a critically searching way. Question 2, on the other hand, asks you to 'evaluate' the role of control in the experience of stress. There are many ways in which you can evaluate material, but one useful way is to examine the degree of research support for a particular assertion. The really high marks are awarded for material that is used effectively. It is well worth bearing this in mind when making your decision which question to choose.

Matthew and Parveen decide to answer Question 1. Their answers are shown next.

(a) What is meant by the terms 'stressor', 'stress inoculation' and 'hardiness'?

[2 marks + 2 marks + 2 marks]

MATTHEW'S ANSWER

A stressor is something that causes stress.

Stress inoculation is where something causes particularly intense stress, such as the death of a spouse.

Hardiness is a measure of personality where you are resistant to stressful situations and are not particularly affected by them.

PARVEEN'S ANSWER

A stressor is something in the environment (such as examinations) that produces a stress response in a person.

This is a way in which people can be trained to deal more effectively with stress. It involves analysing how they have dealt with stress in the past and then using this to deal more effectively with stress in the future.

Hardiness is a set of personality features (control, commitment and challenge) that help you to resist the harmful effects of stress.

(b) Describe **one** physical approach to stress management. [6 marks]

MATTHEW'S ANSWER

One way in which people deal with stress is to take drugs such as beta-blockers which work by altering the way that the brain works. These are commonly taken by musicians and snooker players. Other types of drug are librium and valium which alter the brain's chemistry and so lower the levels of stress experienced by the person. Drugs like librium and valium can make people dependent on them if they are taken for a long period of time so should only be used for short periods of time.

PARVEEN'S ANSWER

One physical approach to stress management is to take drugs that are designed to lower the experience of stress and anxiety. These drugs include anti-anxiety drugs such as benzodiazepine (BZ) and beta-blockers.

BZs work in the same way as neurotransmitters that usually slow down physical arousal in the body. BZs bind with the same receptors in the brain. Another way in which people can lower stress by using drugs is with beta-blockers. These drugs lower the level of sympathetic nervous system arousal in the body.

(c) Give **two** criticisms of the approach you have described in (b). [3 marks + 3 marks]

MATTHEW'S ANSWER

One problem is that people become dependent on drugs and therefore they should only be used for short periods of time. There are two types of dependency, psychological and physical, and if drugs such as librium and valium are used over long periods, people may become both physically and psychologically dependent on them.

Drugs have side effects and may not have much of an effect on the cause of the stress.

PARVEEN'S ANSWER

The long-term use of benzodiazepines may lead to dependency and there is evidence that people's ability to deal with stress declines over time because of this dependency on the drugs.

Because BZs act very quickly and have an almost immediate effect, doctors tend to over-prescribe them and don't really consider their other problems.

How to score full marks

Part (a)

 MATTHEW'S ANSWER

Matthew's definition of a stressor is limited, and makes no reference to the fact that a stressor is **a feature of the environment that produces a stress response** in the individual. He **does** point out that stressors produce stress, so there is understanding that they are the cause of a stress response, therefore he receives 1/2. **His definition of stress inoculation is a nice idea but completely wrong**, so 0/2. Matthew's definition of hardiness is not particularly precise, but is sufficiently accurate for 2/2. He does, for example, stress that it is a type of **personality** that leads to **resistance** to the effects of stress.

PARVEEN'S ANSWER

Parveen's definition of a stressor is accurate and focuses nicely on the two main aspects of this term as detailed above, so **2/2**. Her definition of stress inoculation is accurate and again deals with the main aspects of this technique – that it trains individuals to deal more effectively with stressful situations by helping them to analyse how they have dealt with stress in the past. **She might have mentioned that it is a cognitive-behavioural technique, but the description given is sufficient for 2/2**. Parveen has given the specific set of personality features associated with hardiness (control, commitment and challenge), although this would not be necessary for the full 2 marks. That apart, her answer is very similar to Matthew's, so receives 2/2.

Part (b)

MATTHEW'S ANSWER

Although Matthew has written a fair amount in his response to this question, **much of the content is vague or inappropriate**. The question clearly asks for a **description** of an approach to stress management, so **the evaluation of the use of drugs is clearly irrelevant in this context and would not receive any credit**. It is important in questions such as this to **focus your answer very directly on the specific requirements of the question** rather than simply filling your answer with material that may or may not be relevant. Matthew has correctly identified a physical approach to stress management (the use of drugs), although his description of how such drugs reduce stress is extremely vague. Beta-blockers do more than simply 'altering the way that the brain works'.

PARVEEN'S ANSWER

Parveen has produced a **concise description** of how drugs might be used in stress management. This is an **appropriate approach** and Parveen has produced **an accurate account of the actions of selected anti-anxiety drugs**. There is not a lot more that would be required to gain full marks for this question. Parveen has described the action of BZs (they 'mimic' the actions of neurotransmitters that usually slow down physical arousal in the body). **Her description of the action of beta-blockers is more general and non-specific**. We are told that they 'lower the level of sympathetic nervous system arousal', but we are not told how they do this. **To gain full marks**, Parveen might have added that beta-blockers work by blocking receptors for the neurotransmitter noradrenaline (known as norepinephrine in the US), thus stopping it from activating the sympathetic nervous system.

Part (c)

MATTHEW'S ANSWER

Matthew has provided two appropriate criticisms of the use of drugs in stress management. For his first criticism, he explains that drugs such as librium and valium (BZs) may produce **both physical and psychological dependency** and therefore should only be prescribed for short periods of time. There is probably just enough here for 3 marks, but **he might have done better to have explained what he meant by physical and psychological dependency** in this context. The second criticism is actually two separate criticisms (drugs have **side effects** and they may not have much of an effect on the **cause** of the stress). The second of these is probably the better developed, but even this is **brief and lacks detail**, so would only be worth 1 mark. To have gained full marks for this criticism, Matthew might have added that as drugs affect the individual **physiologically**, they cannot do much for the **causes** of stress, which are usually an aspect of the environment. Drugs work, therefore, as a **palliative** treatment (i.e., they temporarily alleviate the anxiety being experienced) rather than being something that can alter the source of the stress itself.

PARVEEN'S ANSWER

Parveen has given a **good criticism** of the long-term use of benzodiazepines (that this may lead to a reduced ability to deal with stress because of the individual's dependency on the drug). **Her second criticism is less well developed.** BZs are very quick-acting, and perhaps they are over-prescribed because of this, but Parveen does not **elaborate** on her claim that 'their other problems' are overlooked. This second criticism would receive 2 of the 3 marks. To have gained full marks, Parveen should have **explained** that the use of such palliative measures (in this case, drugs) may do nothing to help the individual deal with whatever is causing the stress in the first place (such as overwork or an unsatisfactory relationship).

Don't forget ...

- **Giving example**s in definitions can sometimes add that extra bit of detail to make sure of the full 2 marks.

- If asked to describe **one** approach, don't write about more than one unless they are all parts of the same broad 'approach'. For example, a number of different drugs might be taken to counter the effects of stress, but these all constitute the same basic approach – the use of drugs.

- **When asked for a description, provide some detail**. A definition or short sentence is not enough. Use the marks provided as a guide to how much you should write. Three minutes allows you to write a short paragraph, whereas for six minutes you should be writing twice as much.

- When asked to **describe** or **explain** something, don't waste time evaluating it, as this will not gain you extra marks.

- **When asked for two (or three) of something**, remember that each is marked independently, so don't spend too much time on one to the detriment of the other.

Matthew's answer to Question 1, part (d)

(d) 'Women may live longer than men simply because they react differently to stress.'

To what extent are the effects of stress modified by gender differences? [12 marks]

Quite a good opening. Matthew doesn't waste any time getting into a discussion about the quotation. He has the date wrong (it should be 1976), but doesn't lose any marks for this. It is good that he tries to *explain* why there might be gender differences.

The answer is starting to slow down. It becomes obvious that Matthew has run out of things to say, so he is *recycling the same material* in slightly different forms – this adds very little.

As suspected, Matthew has nothing more to say about gender differences. A speculative opening sentence is followed by material that has nothing to do with gender differences so earns *no more marks*.

Women are thought to live longer than men because they are less physiologically aroused than men when in stressful situations (Frankenhauser et al., 1996). This might be because they make more use of social support networks or it may also mean that there are important physiological differences between men and women.

Men and women might differ in the way their nervous systems react to stressful situations. If men are more aroused by stressful situations this might explain why they don't tend to live as long as women do. Men don't make as much use of social networks and are more likely to keep things bottled up or turn to drink.

Men and women may also have different personalities. Research into personality differences has shown that some people display Type A behaviour, which is characterized by constantly working under time pressure and being more competitive than other people. There is a possibility that people with the Type A behaviour pattern are more likely to show signs of stress-related illness (such as coronary heart disease). This might affect one gender more than the other and so might explain why women tend to live longer than men.

3/12

Parveen's answer to Question 1, part (d)

(d) 'Women may live longer than men simply because they react differently to stress.'

To what extent are the effects of stress modified by gender differences? [12 marks]

A good start, but there is *no need to repeat the question* in this first sentence.

This is a good way to use this study. Parveen *describes* a relevant study, but shows awareness that there are *different* ways of interpreting its findings.

The effects of stress are modified by gender in a number of ways. Stoney et al. (1990) found that women showed much smaller increases in blood pressure compared to men during stressful situations. This might indicate a physiological difference between men and women, with the stress pathways of women being less reactive than men, or alternatively, it may show that men and women differ in their attitude to stressful situations like examinations, with men being more competitive and therefore more aroused by competitive situations.

An interesting study. Parveen has presented a good précis of the Taylor et al. study, although she hasn't said how *males* deal with their stress.

Research by Taylor et al. (2000) has found that males and females respond differently to stress and that this might be the result of evolutionary differences between the sexes. They found that females tend to deal with their stress by seeking social contact and looking after their young, a process that they referred to as 'tending and befriending'.

A good explanation of *why* this difference exists. This lends some scientific credibility to the claims made earlier.

Taylor et al. suggested that this 'tend and befriend' behaviour might be linked to the action of the hormone oxytocin, which is released at times of stress. This has been shown to make both animals and humans calmer and more social. Women appear to have more of this hormone and its action is amplified by the female hormone oestrogen.

A good finale, with Parveen using another researcher's views to *balance* the claim that these differences are biologically determined. There is another reference to 'evolutionary origins', but we aren't told what these are. However, the question does not require an explanation of these, and this is a very *effective* use of 12 minutes so deserves full marks.

Taylor et al. (2000) argue that this gender difference may have evolutionary origins but Eagley (2000) disagrees, saying that different behaviours can be 'learned on the job', so we don't know how much of these gender differences are due to hormonal differences and how many are learned. It is possible that differences in the way that males and females deal with stress have nothing to do with biological factors but are simply a part of the gender-role socialization that males and females experience as they grow up.

12/12

How to score full marks for part (d)

Don't waste time

With 12 marks to earn in a short period, it is important not to waste time. **Give only the information that is asked for**. Remember to **link all your points clearly to the question**. Always remember that this is the **AO2** part of the question (see pages 6–9), so structure your answer accordingly.

Stick to the question

It is **vitally important** in all the questions in this examination that you **stick rigidly to the exact question set**. Matthew does not do this – his exposition of personality differences in the experience of stress was not asked for, is not required and simply does not earn any credit. **It is better to write nothing at all and pass on to the next question than to waste time writing about something that is irrelevant**. Nor is it convincing to speculate, as Matthew does here, that there may be personality differences between the sexes that might account for the different ways in which males and females are affected by arousing situations. This may or may not be the case, but he has no **evidence** or **argument** to back up this suggestion, so really it isn't worth trying to make the link.

Use research evidence effectively

Parveen, on the other hand, **focuses on the question set at all times and constantly engages with the question in a critically searching way**. This is very effective, so we might spend a little time analysing why this was such a good response. First, she looks at claims for gender differences in the light of research evidence. Particularly when answering questions that begin with the instruction 'To what extent…', it is a good idea to **gather evidence** that might **support or challenge** the topic in question. Parveen does this, but Matthew simply makes assertions and does not attempt to back these up with research evidence.

Engage and elaborate

It is not sufficient merely to document gender differences in reactions to stress, but **effective critical commentary also requires you to engage with this material in a meaningful way**. Matthew offers a rather weak point that men may not live as long because 'they are more likely to keep things bottled up or turn to drink', but **fails to elaborate on this or support it at all**. This is a pity, because men **are** more prone to alcohol abuse as well as a number of other stress-related disorders, but we cannot assume that Matthew, from the information given here, knows about such research. Parveen, on the other hand, offers the suggestion that this may be due to the tendency for females to 'tend and befriend' in times of stress. Parveen also offers the fact that males and females differ in their levels of oxytocin, and that the action of this hormone is amplified by the female hormone oestrogen. It is not necessary to know about the actions of oxytocin, but the role suggested here for its action in stress reduction is perfectly reasonable, given the elaborate role played by this hormone in the brain.

Work logically towards a conclusion

Parveen also casts a critical eye over the claims that such differences between the sexes have a **biological** origin. Quoting the views of Alice Eagley, she suggests that differences in the ways that the sexes handle stress may be a product of **socialization** differences rather than biological factors, but it is difficult to disentangle the two. This is a good route through the answer. First, **look at the evidence for gender differences in the effects of stress**. Second, **try to explain the evidence**. Third, **be critical about the different explanations**. Although she does not say as much, it is fairly easy to conclude from Parveen's answer that the effects of stress **are** modified by gender differences, although the **reasons** for these differences cannot be certain.

Don't forget ...

- **Keep yourself focused on the question at all times**. Remember that **irrelevant** information will not gain marks.

- This last part of the question will be assessing your ability to **analyse and evaluate** theories, concepts, studies and methods and to **communicate** your knowledge and understanding of psychology **in a clear and effective manner** (AO2 or Assessment Objective 2).

- When answering questions that begin '**To what extent** ... ', make it obvious that you are reviewing the evidence **critically**. The use of **link words and phrases** such as 'However ...' and '**This conclusion is challenged by** ...' will help to make this obvious.

Key points to remember

Stress

Stress may be seen as an aspect of the environment (the **stressor**) or the body's response to it (the **stress response**). Stress is more usually defined as a **deficit between the perceived demands of a situation and the perceived ability to cope** (the transactional model).

Stress as a bodily response

The body responds to stress in different ways. The main components of the stress response involve the **release of corticosteroids from the adrenal cortex and sympathetic arousal**, leading to increased secretion of adrenaline and noradrenaline from the adrenal medulla. The **General Adaptation Syndrome** was one of the first attempts to show how chronic stress could lead to illness. This has three stages, **alarm** (where the stress response is activated), **resistance** (as the body copes with stress) and **exhaustion** (where stress-related illness may develop). Stress can have **direct detrimental effects on health**, including the development of cardiovascular disorders, and **indirect effects** through the suppression of the immune system.

Sources of stress

Research has identified **life changes** (such as bereavement and divorce) as significant sources of stress, although more recent conceptualizations (such as the 'hassles' scale) have focused on the **minor stressors** of everyday life. The role of the workplace in the development of stress has emphasized a number of **organizational** sources of stress, which apply to most workers. These include relations with co-workers, workload, job insecurity and lack of control. Personality differences in the **reaction** to stress include Type A behaviour, which appears to make people more vulnerable to stress-related illness. Females appear to experience lower levels of stress-related arousal, which also makes them less vulnerable to stress-related illness. Cultures may differ in the degree of **social support** available (such as the use of social networks) and the type of **coping strategies** used to deal with stress.

Critical issue: Stress management

The potentially harmful effects of stress means that effective techniques for **stress management** are essential. Some techniques are **physical** (such as the use of drugs), whilst others are **psychological** (such as meditation). Psychological approaches to stress can either be **general**, such as using relaxation techniques, or meditation to reduce the body's state of arousal, or **specific**, using cognitive and behavioural training. **Meichenbaum's Stress-Inoculation training** has three phases (conceptualization, skills training and practice, real-life application). **Kobasa's notion of 'hardiness'** is taken to mean resistance to illness, or ability to deal with stress. Those who report the fewest illnesses show three kinds of hardiness (challenge, commitment and control).

The effectiveness of a particular technique is also determined by a range of other factors, including **previous experience, individual differences, social support** and **control**.

Question for you to try

Examiner's hints
- The first part of the question asks for **two** ways, therefore **divide your time equally** when answering this part.
- Part (b) asks for an **outline** of research in this area. This calls for a **précis** of research findings, **not a prolonged description** of individual studies.
- Take care that the procedures and conclusions you describe in part (c) are from the **same study**.
- In part (d) you **do not have to refer directly to the quotation**.
- Remember that in part (d) you need to show your **skills in analysing and evaluating** the role of control in the experience of stress.

(a) Outline **two** ways in which the body responds to stress.   [3 marks + 3 marks]

(b) Outline research into the effects of stress on the immune system.   [6 marks]

(c) Describe the procedures and conclusions of **one** research study that has investigated the role of the workplace as a source of stress.   [6 marks]

(d) 'Somehow, when you feel in control of events around you, you don't feel quite as stressed.'

Evaluate the role of 'control' in the experience of stress.   [12 marks]

Answers are given on pp. 86–87.

Exam Questions

Time allowed: 30 minutes

Answer **one** question. You should attempt all parts of the question you choose.

Question 1

(a) Outline **two** attempts to define psychological abnormality.   [3 marks + 3 marks]

(b) Outline the clinical characteristics of bulimia nervosa.   [6 marks]

(c) Describe the procedures *and* findings from any **one** study that has investigated either anorexia nervosa **and/or** bulimia nervosa.   [6 marks]

(d) 'Psychological abnormality can only be explained by considering a combination of psychological and biological factors.'

To what extent does the biological (medical) model adequately account for the causes of psychological abnormality?   [12 marks]

Question 2

(a) Give **two** limitations of the 'statistical infrequency' definition of abnormality.   [3 marks + 3 marks]

(b) Outline the major implications for treatment according to any **two** models of abnormality.   [6 marks + 6 marks]

(c) 'There is little evidence that eating disorders are caused by underlying biological factors.'

Consider the view that eating disorders can be explained in purely psychological terms.   [12 marks]

CHOOSING THE BEST QUESTION

● Take time to read both questions carefully, even though time is limited. **You will need to check what is in all parts of both questions before you can decide which question gives you the best opportunity to show what you know.** All the topic areas in the 'Individual Difference' section (i.e., 'Defining psychological abnormality', 'Biological and psychological models of abnormality' and 'Eating disorders') will be sampled across the two questions, but **this will not necessarily be the case within one question. You need to look carefully to see whether any topic area has been omitted** because this could be an important factor in making up your mind.

● In this example, **both questions sample all the topic areas, but the way in which the marks are distributed is different.** You may, for example, prefer to answer Question 2, which has only three parts, rather than Question 1, which has four. (Remember, however, that **each question has a total of 30 marks.**)

● Question 1, part (a) asks you to outline **any two attempts** to define psychological abnormality, so you can choose the two about which you feel most confident. Question 2, part (a), on the other hand, forces you to consider **only** the 'statistical infrequency' definition. However, **beware** of leaping into Question 1 because of this. If you look at part (b), you will find that it is Question 2 that offers you the choice, whereas Question 1 ties you specifically into your knowledge about bulimia nervosa.

● Think carefully about the specific wording of questions. Question 1, part (c), for example, requires a description of the procedures **and** findings from an eating disorder study. If you only know about the procedures, but can remember nothing about the findings of such a study, you will lose marks. In this case, it might be better to consider Question 2, provided that you feel competent to outline the implications for treatment of **two** models of abnormality. **You need to think carefully about the relative weighting of the marks in the two questions.**

● **It is very important to look at the last part of each question carefully.** Whether this is part (d), as in Question 1, or part (c), as in Question 2, the **last part is always assessed for your ability to analyse and evaluate** (AO2) and is always worth 12 marks. AO2 is a different skill from AO1 (knowledge and understanding) and **you will need to think carefully about which of the two questions will allow you to demonstrate this skill to your best advantage.** In this example, both questions require you to be able to consider causal explanations of abnormal disorders. However, in Question 2, you have to look at a **specific area of abnormal psychology** (i.e., eating disorders), whereas in Question 1, you can look at a **broader range of disorders** of your own choosing.

Laura and Luke decide to answer Question 1. Their answers are shown next.

(a) Outline **two** attempts to define psychological abnormality.　　　[3 marks + 3 marks]

LAURA'S ANSWER

One way of defining abnormality is to say that people are failing to function properly. This is considered to be the most humane way of defining abnormality. Another way is when you deviate from social norms. Social norms are a bit like rules set down by society. If you do not follow these rules, you are abnormal. Rules are like not having babies outside marriage or being in a homosexual relationship although some of these rules change over time.

LUKE'S ANSWER

One definition is the medical model which is a biological approach. According to this, all psychological abnormality has a physical cause. Some mental disorders have a clear physical cause like alcohol poisoning or brain tumour but the cause of other disorders, like schizophrenia, has not yet been clearly identified.

Another definition is called deviation from mental health. This is where you are considered abnormal if you don't have all the characteristics of a mentally healthy person like being positive and able to adapt. However, this would be very difficult for most of us.

(b) Outline the clinical characteristics of bulimia nervosa.　　　[6 marks]

LAURA'S ANSWER

There are two main eating disorders, anorexia and bulimia. They are becoming more common and sometimes affect famous people like Princess Diana. Anorexia means loss of appetite but this is not quite right because people with anorexia are often hungry although they do not eat enough. Bulimia is different because they eat a lot and then vomit. They don't die of starvation but they damage their bodies e.g. their teeth go bad and they get puffy faces.

LUKE'S ANSWER

Bulimia occurs mainly in women and often follows on from anorexia. They do not lose weight like people with anorexia, but they have funny ideas about their body shape. They eat lots of food because they are stressed but then feel guilty and try to lose the weight they have put on. They do this by being sick or by taking laxatives and other medicines. This can damage their teeth and kidneys and can cause stomach and bowel problems. They also often do lots of exercise to try and lose weight. Some people think that bulimia is caused by social pressures and by the media and others think that it is related to early sexual abuse.

(c) Describe the procedures *and* findings from any **one** study that has investigated either anorexia nervosa **and/or** bulimia nervosa.   [6 marks]

LAURA'S ANSWER

Holland did a study on anorexia in twins. He found that the rate for identical twins was higher than the rate for non-identical twins. Another study was done on bulimia in twins and they also found the rate was higher for identical twins.

LUKE'S ANSWER

Fairburn et al. did a study on eating disorders. It was a very large study in which they compared people with eating disorders with other people. There were about 150 people in each group and they were all interviewed to find out things about their attitudes and their backgrounds. Fairburn found out certain things from the interview tapes. For example, people with eating disorders were perfectionist and they had low opinions of themselves.

How to score full marks

Part (a)

LAURA'S ANSWER

Laura has chosen two perfectly acceptable definitions of abnormality, but **she has not provided the appropriate level of detail in her outlines**. She has **identified** the 'failure to function adequately' definition, **but has really done little other than to name it**. The statement that it is a 'humane way of defining abnormality' is not **explained** and is, in any case, more of an evaluation than a description. This answer can only be awarded 1 mark. **For full marks, the answer needed to be more detailed and to explain exactly what is meant by a failure to function adequately**. It would have been useful to include an **example**, e.g. a depressed person who cannot sleep or concentrate and who has to take time off work.

Laura is a bit more successful with her second outline definition. She identifies the 'deviation from social norms' definition and explains what social norms are, giving appropriate, though dated, examples. She indicates that social norms differ over time, but **she does not make the point clearly that these changing norms affect judgements about abnormality**.

LUKE'S ANSWER

Luke has, unfortunately, misunderstood the requirements of the question. **This highlights the importance of knowing the specification and making sure that you understand the basic terminology**. Luke has described a **model of abnormality rather than a definition and so can earn no marks for his first answer**. He has, however, identified an appropriate definition (i.e., deviation from mental health) for his second answer and has outlined this reasonably accurately. **His last sentence contains an evaluation of the definition rather than an outline, and so gains no marks**.

Part (b)

LAURA'S ANSWER

Laura has made the mistake here of introducing irrelevant material. The question is specifically related to bulimia nervosa and not to eating disorders in general. Thus, **she earns no credit for her comments about anorexia nervosa**. Her outline of the characteristics of bulimia is limited and fairly basic, and just about manages to earn her 2 marks.

LUKE'S ANSWER

Note that **characteristics do not simply mean symptoms**. It would be perfectly acceptable to include information on the **incidence and prevalence** of bulimia as well as symptoms and consequences, since all these factors contribute to the clinical picture of the disorder. Luke has recognized this and has provided information about the fact that bulimia occurs more frequently in women and that it often affects people who have already suffered from anorexia. He outlines some of the symptoms, although he could have provided more detail here, and then indicates some of the consequences of the behaviour associated with bulimia, i.e., the fact that purging and vomiting can give rise to physical damage. **The material he uses is accurate and relevant, although not always well detailed**. However, the last sentence, where he offers possible causes of bulimia, is not relevant and does not gain any marks. **Note that he will not have marks deducted for including irrelevant material, but that he penalizes himself in terms of wasted time**.

Part (c)

LAURA'S ANSWER

Laura has chosen an appropriate study but, unfortunately, **does not seem to have enough knowledge about it to answer the question adequately**. She mentions that the study was carried out on twins, which is a very weak and basic reference to procedure, and then provides a muddled sentence on the findings. For example, it is unclear what she means by 'the rate'. **She could have avoided this lack of clarity by simply adding the word 'concordance' before rate.**

It is sometimes difficult to give equal weighting to a description of the procedures and findings in a given study and you will find that this is not necessary. The important thing is that you include some description of both aspects. It is unlikely, for example, that you will know the exact details of how Holland et al. conducted their study, but you must include some reference to the basic procedure. Note that this could include the type of sample used. For example, you could write: 'Holland et al. conducted a study on sets of female twins who had been selected because one of the pair had been diagnosed with anorexia nervosa. Some of the twin pairs were monozygotic (MZ) and some were dizygotic (DZ). Holland et al. confirmed this relationship by using blood tests. They then investigated the other member of the twin pair to find out the concordance rate of anorexia.' Note that the use of specialist terms (e.g. *MZ* and *DZ twins* and the *concordance rate*) allows you to express ideas succinctly. You do not need to explain these specialist terms. As far as the findings are concerned, it is useful if you can remember more detail than Laura has provided. For example, in one study, Holland et al. found a concordance rate of 56 per cent in MZ twins compared with only 7 per cent in DZ twins. Moreover, in three cases where the twins did not have anorexia, there was evidence of her having another psychological disorder. Note that Holland and his colleagues conducted more than one study on the genetic basis of anorexia. When you answer questions like these, you should make sure that you do not muddle the details of two separate studies.

Laura has tried to pad out her answer by referring to a second study carried out to investigate the genetic basis of bulimia. This is not a sensible strategy and Laura is simply wasting time. The question requires a description of one study and no credit will be given for a description of another one. Her answer gains only 1 mark.

LUKE'S ANSWER

Luke has chosen a completely different kind of study and has been more successful in his description. The question is broad-ranging and allows a wide choice of studies – any study of anorexia nervosa and/or bulimia nervosa could be described, whether it concerns causal factors, incidence or treatment. Luke has accurately named the researcher who carried out this particular study and has correctly stated that the research was based on interviews. He has remembered that people with eating disorders were compared with other people, but his description would have been more detailed if he had recalled the nature of the comparison groups, i.e., one group of people with other kinds of psychological disorder and one group of mentally healthy people. He has not been quite accurate about the numbers in each group, although the precise numbers would not be required for full marks. He has accurately stated the findings, although he has not made it explicitly clear that the people with anorexia differed from the other groups. As it is, he earns 4/6 marks.

Don't forget ...

- Make sure that you understand the terms used in the specification. If you are asked for a definition of abnormality, you will gain no marks if you describe a model.

- Look carefully at the mark allocation at the end of each question part. There are 3 marks for each outline of a definition in part (a), but 6 marks for the outline of the characteristics of bulimia in part (b). Although an outline is required in both cases, you clearly need to include more detail in part (b) than in part (a).

- If asked to give an outline of the characteristics of a specific disorder, do not waste time describing other disorders. You will gain no marks by doing this.

- If you are asked to describe the procedures and findings of a study, you must choose one where you can accurately recall these details.

- If you are asked to describe one study, do not waste time describing other studies. You will gain no marks for this.

Laura's answer to Question 1, part (d)

(d) 'Psychological abnormality can only be explained by considering a combination of psychological and biological factors.'

To what extent does the biological (medical) model adequately account for the causes of psychological abnormality? [12 marks]

> **Laura is describing the medical model here rather than answering the question. She could have used some of this material *more effectively* to make an evaluative point, i.e., that the medical model can explain some disorders better than others.**

The medical model sees psychological abnormality as a disease. For example, general paresis is known to be caused by syphilis. Other disorders like depression do not have a definite cause at the moment but the medical model thinks that a physical cause will be found. Physical causes can be genetic or to do with neurotransmitters in the brain or because of brain damage e.g. a head injury.

> **Phrases such as 'a good model' are *too vague*. Laura makes valid comments about 'no blame' and 'labelling', but fails to draw a *relevant* evaluative point.**

It is a good model because it takes away blame from the individual. The person is seen as ill rather than evil. There is a problem that people get labelled with an illness e.g. schizophrenia.

> **Laura is hinting at a sound evaluative point here, i.e., that the medical model can account only for certain aspects of psychological abnormality, but, again, she does not make the *explicit* link to causal explanations.**

The medical model uses drugs to treat mental illness. This can be good for people with depression because it may prevent suicide but it does not stop them being unhappy with their lives. They probably need counselling to help them as well.

People with schizophrenia have problems with certain neurotransmitters in the brain but this could be caused by the drugs and not by the illness.

> **This is a reasonable point – it refers to the difficulty of disentangling cause and effect – but, as before, the point is not made very *clearly*.**

The medical model accounts for the causes of psychological disorders quite well but there are other models that give different points of view.

> **This is a weak concluding statement. Other models could be used effectively to evaluate the medical model, but Laura only hints at this.**

4/12

Luke's answer to Question 1, part (d)

(d) 'Psychological abnormality can only be explained by considering a combination of psychological and biological factors.'

To what extent does the biological (medical) model adequately account for the causes of psychological abnormality?   [12 marks]

> **Although the differences between psychiatrists and psychologists is not quite as clear-cut as this, Luke makes *relevant* commentary here about other possible causes of psychological abnormality. He addresses the question by stating that no single model offers an adequate explanation.**

The biological model is the model usually preferred by doctors. They believe that mental illness is the same as physical illness. Many psychologists, on the other hand, think that psychological disorders are caused by factors such as the environment. It is probably true to say that biological and environmental factors both have a part to play. No model on its own can account for all types of psychological abnormality.

> **Another relevant point, *although it is not supported by evidence*.**

There are some psychological disorders where the physical cause seems clear. General paresis, for example, is caused by syphilis but researchers have not yet found the physical reason for some disorders. They are more likely to be caused by other things like stress or bad treatment as a child.

> **This is a related but separate point, i.e. that a single disorder might have more than one underlying cause.**

It is also possible that a single disorder could be caused by different things and not just biological factors. Depression might be partly caused by faulty neurotransmitters in the brain but only in people who are also having bad life experiences.

> **There are *two* valid points here, but the commentary is *limited*.**

If the medical model is right, then people with psychological disorders should get better with drugs. Some people get better but not everyone. Also sometimes the drugs themselves cause problems in the brain and it is difficult to know what came first.

> **Again, Luke makes a valid point but does not relate it *clearly* to the question. He then wastes time by repeating an idea already expressed. It is better to avoid phrases like: 'As I said before ...'**

Genetics are important in the medical model and some disorders are thought to be passed on from parents. It is difficult to investigate this because families share the same environment as well as the same genes. As I said at the beginning of the essay, I think that psychological disorders are caused by a mixture of psychological and environmental factors.

7/12

How to score full marks for part (d)

Avoid irrelevant material

You only have approximately 12 minutes to answer this question, so **you cannot afford to waste time on irrelevant material**. Laura, for example, has written an introductory paragraph that is poorly focused on the requirements of the question. **She describes the basic assumption of the medical model instead of assessing the adequacy of the model**. She could, however, have used some of this same material to make a valid evaluative point, i.e., 'Research has demonstrated clearly that certain disorders, e.g. general paresis, have underlying physical causes, but it is not so clear-cut for other disorders like anorexia where behavioural or psychodynamic explanations may be more plausible.'

Relate evaluative points to the question

In her second paragraph, **Laura makes two evaluative points about the medical model but does not relate them to the question**, even though they could be made relevant. For example, by explaining psychological disorders in terms of illness, supporters of the medical model operate within a scientific framework, which encourages research. So, even though physical causes have not yet been found for all psychological disorders, it could be argued that research will eventually uncover them. On the other hand, the label of 'mental illness' can prevent people from looking for different, non-biological causes and so may give an unbalanced picture.

Make your evaluative points clear

Laura is slightly more focused in her next paragraph, **but she still does not make her evaluative point entirely clear**. The key point here is that biological treatments, e.g. drugs, have been shown to be effective in disorders such as depression. This lends weight to the idea that the underlying cause is also biological. However, drugs do not always work effectively and do not bring about a complete cure in people who are depressed. This suggests that other factors, such as life circumstances, might contribute to the origin of the disorder.

Use your material effectively

The last two paragraphs are similar in that they hint at evaluation without being explicit. **This is such a pity because Laura has some good material throughout her answer, but she has not used it effectively to address the question**.

Use evidence to support your arguments

Luke has used very similar material in his answer, but he has managed to adapt it better to the requirements of the question. **The reason that he has not achieved higher marks is that his analysis is slightly limited and he has not always supported his arguments with evidence or examples**.

Consider strengths and weaknesses

In this type of question, **you need to consider both the strengths and the weaknesses of the model in order to be able to assess the extent to which it is effective**. However, **make sure that your evaluative comments are clearly linked to the question**. For example, it is a valid criticism of the model to say that it encourages people with psychological disorders to become passive and dependent. On its own, however, this statement does not help us to decide whether the model adequately accounts for the causes of psychological disorders and so would not gain any marks.

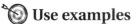 Use examples

It is unlikely that you will know about many specific studies in this area, but **it is important to try to support your arguments where possible**, e.g. by using examples. For example, Luke gained credit for his argument that certain disorders are better explained in psychological terms. **However, he would have made the point more powerfully if he had given anorexia nervosa as an example of such a disorder**. Similarly, he could have illustrated his point about genetic research by writing something like: 'Twin and family studies have provided support for the idea that certain disorders such as schizophrenia are transmitted genetically. However, social learning theorists would argue that family members often share the same environment as well as the same genes and might develop psychological disorders through modelling people around them.'

Don't forget ...

- The **last part** of all AS questions (except for 'Research Methods') is worth 12 marks, so **allow yourself adequate time (approximately 12 minutes) to answer it in sufficient detail**.

- This last part of the question will assess your ability to **analyse and evaluate** theories, concepts, studies and methods and to **communicate** your knowledge and understanding of psychology **in a clear and effective manner** (AO2 or Assessment Objective 2). **You will not gain marks here for simply describing models or research**.

- **Make your evaluative points clear and relevant**. Do not leave it up to the examiner to guess the point you are making – the examiner will not make the appropriate links for you.

- Remember that you need to **consider both sides of the argument** when you are asked to assess the extent to which a theory/model is supported.

- **Two marks are allocated for the quality of written communication** shown in a paper. It is worthwhile trying to write clearly and accurately, using specialist terms correctly.

Abnormality

Abnormality is one topic within the area of individual differences. The term **psychological abnormality** refers to behaviours and psychological functioning which are considered to be different from normal. **There is no agreement as to the precise definition of the term abnormality and various suggestions have been put forward**.

Biological and psychological models of abnormality

Models of abnormality offer explanations about the origins of psychological disorders and also have implications for their treatment. According to the **biological (medical)** model, psychological disorders are illnesses caused by biological factors and should be treated with physical treatments, e.g. drugs. The **psychodynamic** model is a psychological model first developed by **Freud**, who believed that mental disorders arose from unresolved, unconscious conflicts experienced in childhood. The main goal of psychodynamic therapy is to enable individuals to access their repressed anxieties and conflicts and to resolve them. Another psychological model was put forward by the **behaviourists**. The basic assumption of this model is that all behaviour, including maladaptive or abnormal behaviour, is learned through processes such as classical and operant conditioning. Treatment involves further conditioning designed to remove the maladaptive behaviours. The central assumption of the **cognitive** model is that psychological disorders arise from irrational and distorted thinking patterns. Cognitive therapy aims to alter faulty thinking and replace it with more rational and positive beliefs.

Defining psychological abnormality

There have been many attempts to define the term 'psychological abnormality'. According to one definition, any behaviour that is **statistically infrequent** is seen as abnormal. A problem with this definition concerns the desirability of a particular behaviour or psychological ability. It is statistically rare to be classified as a genius, but this could be seen as a desirable quality and does not indicate clinical abnormality. The concept of **deviation from social norms** takes this factor into account and behaviour is judged to be abnormal if it contravenes accepted rules within a society. A rather different way of defining abnormality is in terms of **deviation from ideal mental health**. **Jahoda** identified a list of six characteristics which she believed defined mental health. An individual who does not demonstrate these characteristics is thought to be vulnerable to psychological problems. One limitation of this definition lies in the difficulty of measuring these characteristics. The fourth definition to be considered is the **failure to function adequately**. According to this approach, people behave abnormally when they fail to cope with everyday aspects of their life such as going to work or enjoying leisure time. **A major limitation of all the definitions is that they are culture-bound**. Behaviour that is acceptable to one group of people and at one period in history may be unacceptable to others.

Critical issue: eating disorders – anorexia nervosa and bulimia nervosa

The most common eating disorders are **anorexia nervosa** and **bulimia nervosa**. Anorexia is characterized by very low body weight, distorted body image and severely restricted food intake, whereas bulimia is characterized by episodes of secret binge eating followed by purging. Various explanations have been put forward to account for these disorders. **Biological explanations** include infection, hormonal imbalance and genetic transmission, but evidence for such factors is not strong. **Psychodynamic explanations** include avoidance of sexual maturity, sexual abuse and breakdowns in family dynamics. There is some support for such theories but research is limited. **Behaviourists** explain eating disorders in terms of **conditioning** and **modelling**. The fact that the incidence of eating disorders appears to differ across cultures lends some support to this view.

Question for you to try

Q2

(a) Give **two** limitations of the 'statistical infrequency' definition of abnormality.

[3 marks + 3 marks]

(b) Outline the major implications for treatment according to any **two** models of abnormality. [6 marks + 6 marks]

(c) 'There is little evidence that eating disorders are caused by underlying biological factors.'

Consider the view that eating disorders can be explained in purely psychological terms. [12 marks]

Answers are given on pp. 88–90.

Exam Questions

Time allowed: 30 minutes

Answer **one** question. You should attempt all parts of the question you choose.

Question 1

(a) Describe **two** psychological processes that might be involved in conformity.

[3 marks + 3 marks]

(b) Outline **two** explanations of why people sometimes do not conform to majority influence.

[3 marks + 3 marks]

(c) Describe the findings *and* conclusions of **one** study of obedience.   [6 marks]

(d) 'Ethical issues are a major concern within psychology.'

Evaluate how psychologists have dealt with the ethical issues raised by research into social influence.   [12 marks]

Question 2

(a) Explain what is meant by the terms 'social influence', 'minority influence' and 'ethical issues'.   [2 marks + 2 marks + 2 marks]

(b) Describe the procedures *and* findings from **one** study of minority influence.

[6 marks]

(c) Outline **two** ways in which minorities exert their influence.

[3 marks + 3 marks]

(d) 'The controversy surrounding research by Milgram and Zimbardo was caused largely by the unpalatable nature of their findings: situations, not personal character, cause people to behave the way they do.'

To what extent are the ethical objections levelled against social influence research, such as that carried out by Milgram and Zimbardo, justified?

[12 marks]

CHOOSING THE BEST QUESTION

Be sure to read both questions carefully before you start writing. In this way you will select the question that will enable you to score the highest marks. **Do a rough calculation to work out how many marks in each question you think you can achieve**. Don't just make up your mind on the basis of the first couple of parts in each question. Which of the questions on page 1 would you choose?

Although all topic areas in 'Social Influence' will be sampled over the two questions, this will not necessarily occur within any one question. **Take care not to rush into answering a question just because the first couple of parts are about an area you particularly enjoyed**. Later parts may ask you about another area altogether. Question 1 begins with two questions on conformity, but part (c) deals with obedience and part (d) concerns ethical issues. Of course, sometimes a question will deal with only one or two topics.

Whether or not you have preferences for individual topics, **you will still need to read each part of the two questions carefully and note their specific requirements**. In Question 2, for example, part (b) asks you to describe the **procedures** and **findings** from one study of minority influence. If you know nothing about the procedures of studies in this area,

then you will be at a disadvantage if you answer Question 2. Question 1, part (c), on the other hand, asks for **findings** and **conclusions** (not procedures) about one study of obedience.

It is important to look at the last part of each question before choosing which to answer. The last part of a question **always** assesses your ability to **analyse and evaluate** (AO2). This is a different skill from AO1 (knowledge and understanding), which is assessed in the other parts of the question. In this case, the last part of both questions deals with ethical issues. Question 1 asks you to **evaluate** the ways in which psychologists have tried to deal with ethical issues that arise from social influence research. Question 2, on the other hand, is different. It asks you to **weigh up the arguments for and against** the ethical objections made against social influence research. Therefore the **focus** of each question is different:

Question 1 focus: Evaluate attempts to deal with ethical issues.

Question 2 focus: Judge whether ethical objections to social influence research are justified.

Sarah and Sam decide to answer Question 1. Their answers are shown next.

(a) Describe **two** psychological processes that might be involved in conformity.

[3 marks + 3 marks]

SARAH'S ANSWER

People might conform because they want to be accepted by their friends or because they are afraid that they might be rejected if they don't.

SAM'S ANSWER

One reason is because of normative social influence. They want to appear normal.

Another reason is because people are sometimes unsure of what to do.

(b) Outline **two** explanations of why people sometimes do not conform to majority influence.

[3 marks + 3 marks]

SARAH'S ANSWER

Sometimes people don't like the group they are with and so they will not agree with them.

Because some people just want to be different from everybody else.

SAM'S ANSWER

If people feel very confident that they are right about something they won't be persuaded to change their minds and conform even if a majority disagrees with them.

I don't think I would conform to majority influence if I thought what they did was wrong.

(c) Describe the findings *and* conclusions of **one** study of obedience. [6 marks]

SARAH'S ANSWER

Milgram invited volunteers to come to his lab to take part in an experiment about learning and memory. When the men arrived at the lab they sat at a shock generator and gave shocks to another man when he gave wrong answers. Most volunteers gave shocks up to

450 volts even though the 'learner' screamed to be let out and even stopped answering altogether. Women also gave shocks when told to do so. The conclusions from this study are that people will give shocks to other people if someone in authority tells them to. 3/6

SAM'S ANSWER

In one study of obedience a doctor phoned and asked a nurse to give a drug to a patient before he arrived. This broke hospital rules. Most nurses began to give the drug (a harmless substance really) until they were stopped by another nurse. The conclusion from this study is that nurses cannot be trusted and will do whatever doctors ask them to. In another study looking at obedience in nurses it was found that most of them disobeyed. Therefore sometimes nurses can be trusted. 2/6

How to score full marks

Part (a)

SARAH'S ANSWER

Sarah's answer describes **only one process**, conforming in order to be liked or accepted (normative social influence). **Her point about conforming to avoid rejection is another way of describing the same process, and so cannot gain marks as a second process**. This is why she scores 0/3 for this. **Remember, for full marks a description needs to be both accurate and detailed**. Sarah scores only 2/3 for describing the first process. As appropriate detail, you could include in your answer that people who yield to normative social influence do not usually change their private opinions, just the opinions they express in public. There are several other processes that could be included as the second one, including informational social influence, mindlessness, social pressure or fear of appearing foolish.

SAM'S ANSWER

Sam's answer does refer to two processes, but **neither is sufficiently detailed for full marks**. He names normative social influence but does not describe it beyond recycling the word 'normative'. The second part of his answer attempts to describe informational social influence, but the description is basic and lacks detail. Therefore he scores 1/3 for each process. **For full marks he needs to show more understanding**. Giving an **example** could do this. For instance, if you attend a classical music concert for the first time, you may not know when to applaud and so would take your lead from others around you. You assume they have more knowledge about how to behave in this situation, which is novel for you. This is an example of **informational social influence**. Dressing like our friends in order to fit in and be accepted is an example of **normative social influence**.

Part (b)

SARAH'S ANSWER

Both parts of Sarah's answer lack detail and each scores only 1/3. For full marks she could have explained that if people do not identify with a group and, therefore, do not use it as a positive reference source, they are unlikely to conform to its views. **To gain full marks for the second part of her answer Sarah could have explained how some people are anti-conformist and always oppose the majority view.** Nevertheless, these anti-conformists usually conform to other, less popular (minority) views or codes. Other explanations you could outline to explain why people do not always conform include desire for individuation or for control. Another explanation forms the first part of Sam's answer.

SAM'S ANSWER

The first part of Sam's answer is accurate and would have been given full marks if it had been more detailed, e.g., explaining **when** people are likely to feel confident enough to resist majority influence. For example, Perrin and Spencer's study showed that engineering students did not conform on a line-length task supposedly because the technical expertise acquired on their course made them confident to judge line lengths. In a question like this, **refer to a specific psychological study wherever possible**. As it is, Sam's answer earns only 2/3. **The second part of Sam's answer gains no marks because it expresses a personal opinion and fails to demonstrate any psychological knowledge.**

Part (c)

SARAH'S ANSWER

Sarah wastes time describing (not entirely accurately) Milgram's procedures. First, you should describe the **findings** of the study (e.g. 65 per cent of participants 'gave shocks' up to 450 volts; no one stopped before 300 volts; under which conditions obedience rates increased and decreased). Next you should describe the **conclusions** (e.g. situational factors are largely responsible for obedience; the majority of ordinary people will obey even when this goes against conscience). **Note that Sarah gives only one conclusion, when the question requires at least two.**

SAM'S ANSWER

Sam has given the correct finding from Hofling's obedience study, but once again he needs to provide more detail (e.g. the exact percentage of nurses who obeyed; that all the telephone conversations with the 'doctor' were short; that nurses reported often being asked to break hospital rules). Neither of the conclusions given is valid, going well beyond what can be concluded from one limited study. You could conclude that in 1966 nurses were inclined to obey a medical authority figure rather too readily and that obedience can be demonstrated in real-life situations as well as in a laboratory. **Note that Sam's reference to 'another study' gains no marks, as only one study was required by the question.**

Don't forget ...

- If asked to describe **more than one** process or explanation, be sure to do so. Try to do each in appropriate detail, as each will be marked independently.

- If asked for information about **one** study, write about only one study!

- **When asked for a description, provide some detail**. A definition or short sentence is not enough. However, remember that you have only got three minutes approximately for a 3-mark answer.

- When choosing a study to describe, take care to select one about which you know enough of the **right sort of detail**.

- **Look out for plurals** in a question, such as finding**s** or conclusion**s**.

Sarah's answer to Question 1, part (d)

(d) 'Ethical issues are a major concern within psychology.'

Evaluate how psychologists have dealt with the ethical issues raised by research into social influence. [12 marks]

What is meant by the term 'ethical'? Wastes time asking a question which cannot be answered. Chatty style is inappropriate.

Psychologists have to be careful to carry out their research in an ethical way. How would you like to be tricked into giving shocks to someone and maybe thinking you'd killed them?

Getting there – three ethical issues mentioned: protection from harm; deception; right of withdrawal.

Milgram and Zimbardo have been criticized for not taking enough care of their participants. Milgram did not tell them the truth. He deceived them so they thought they were taking part in a study about memory. He insisted they carry on giving shocks even when they wanted to stop.

Good. Sarah mentions use of guidelines to deal with ethical issues, *but still no evaluation*. Content of guidelines is not entirely accurate.

Psychologists use guidelines today that stop them deceiving participants. They also have to let participants leave any time they want.

Oh dear, Sarah is wasting time describing Zimbardo's study. This earns no marks. *Still no evaluation.*

In Zimbardo's prison study he had some students arrested at their homes without warning and kept as prisoners. Other students acted as their guards to keep them under control. They began to abuse the prisoners. One prisoner broke down and had to be let out. This is not ethical. You cannot keep people locked up in psychology experiments nowadays.

In total, four ethical guidelines listed but *no evaluation* given.

Psychology guidelines say you have to tell participants the truth, debrief them, get their consent and protect them. If psychologists do this, their research will be ethical.

4/12

63

Sam's answer to Question 1, part (d)

(d) 'Ethical issues are a major concern within psychology.'

Evaluate how psychologists have dealt with the ethical issues raised by research into social influence. [12 marks]

Good start, but Sam needs to *explain* term 'ethical issues'.

Ethical issue of deception identified. Lack of *fully* informed consent hinted at, but not made explicit.

> The research of social psychologists such as Milgram and Zimbardo and Asch raised several ethical issues. Milgram and Asch deceived their participants about the real purpose of their research. Zimbardo's participants knew they had volunteered for a prison simulation study but they did not know whether they would be guards or prisoners.

Sam gets to grips with how psychologists have tried to deal with issue of deception.

Good evaluative point.

> Since these studies, psychologists have developed sets of guidelines to prevent participants being deceived unless it is really necessary. One way to avoid deceiving people is to tell them everything about the study and ask them to role-play as if they had not been told. Generally, however, using role-play gives results different from those found when participants are naive. So this attempt to deal with deception is not altogether successful.

Still on deception. Sam knows a lot about this but should be moving on to another issue.

> Another way to get around deceiving participants is to use only those people who previously have said that they do not mind being deceived. This is called prior general consent.

Presumably running out of time, Sam briefly mentions other ethical issues covered in the guidelines and *makes one evaluative point, but not very clearly.* He would make a better point by adding that the threat of expulsion from the BPS is a powerful incentive for psychologists to adhere to the guidelines.

> BPS guidelines say that participants should be protected from harm, should give fully informed consent before a procedure starts and be debriefed at the end. Psychologists who ignore the guidelines can be expelled from the BPS.

6/12

How to score full marks for part (d)

Answer the question set

With 12 marks to earn in a short period, it is important not to waste time. **Give only the information that is asked for**. Where possible, use **psychological terminology**. This will enable you to write succinctly and help you to **communicate in a clear and effective manner**. Remember to **link all your points clearly to the question**. Always remember that this is the AO2 part of the question (see pages 6–9), so structure your answer accordingly and engage from the start with **evaluating** how psychologists have dealt with ethical issues raised by social influence research.

Avoid rhetorical questions

Avoid asking the examiner questions (as Sarah did). Your job is to answer questions, not ask them! In answering this question, there is no need to give procedural details of studies. Sarah in particular falls into this trap. You are asked to 'evaluate how psychologists have dealt with ethical issues'. **Briefly explain what is meant by an ethical issue**, i.e., a concern about what is considered right or acceptable.

Identify key ethical issues

Quickly **identify** some of the issues thrown up by social influence research, e.g. whether deception can ever be justified, the need for informed consent, the protection of participants, the right to withdraw.

How psychologists deal with ethical issues

Next, look at how psychologists have tried to deal with these issues, e.g. by developing guidelines, setting up ethical committees and by using different research methods such as role-playing and by the use of presumptive consent, prior consent, and the problems that arise from these procedures. Mention these so that it is clear what you are evaluating. However, **do not spend too long describing them**. Your answer needs to be **properly balanced** (this is where Sam fell down badly) and you are primarily required to **show your skills of evaluation** here.

Evaluation

Now to the main part of the question. To evaluate means to '**make an informed judgement by considering strengths and/or weaknesses about**'. You could consider to what extent you think the BPS ethical guidelines provide adequate safeguards. For example, if psychologists infringe the code, they may well be expelled from the BPS. You might also consider **what factors could affect the effectiveness of the ethics committees** who make decisions about the suitability of research projects. The **composition** of ethics committees (whether they contain lay members) and **how rigorously they operate** are important factors. Some people argue that dependence on centralized sets of rules removes responsibility from individual researchers, who may conduct inferior research just because an ethics committee did not stop it. **Codes of conduct and ethical guidelines, therefore, do not guarantee high ethical standards**. Standards are influenced also by those who are on the committees and by how rigorously the guidelines are enforced. Note also that all A level psychology students carry out a research study, very few of which will be scrutinized by an ethics committee. You might also note that at any given time **different countries are using different sets of guidelines**. Furthermore, **guidelines are revised regularly** in order to reflect changes in society's views and so no single set of guidelines provides a universal or absolute truth about what is the right way to conduct research.

Other ways to score full marks …

In addition (or as an alternative) to evaluating the effectiveness of guidelines and ethical committees, **you could also evaluate some of the problems of trying to adhere to guidelines while still carrying out research that is meaningful and valuable**. The use of role-play, for example, as an alternative to deception does not usually produce the same results as those found by Asch and Milgram. **You could also consider the problems of trying to weigh up the relative cost of doing research** (e.g. potential harm to participants) **against the potential benefits to society**. As you can see, there is more than one way of providing a thorough and effective answer to this question.

Don't forget …

- The **last part** of all AS questions (except for 'Research Methods') is **worth 12 marks**, so allow yourself adequate time (approximately 12 minutes) to answer it in sufficient depth.

- This last part of the question will be assessing your ability to **analyse and evaluate** theories, concepts, studies and methods and to **communicate** your knowledge and understanding of psychology **in a clear and effective manner** (AO2 or Assessment Objective 2).

- **Two marks are allocated for the quality of written communication** shown in a paper. It is worthwhile trying to write clearly and accurately, using specialist terms correctly.

Social influence

Social influence refers to the way in which other people affect a person's **attitudes** and **behaviour**. There are different types of social influence, including **majority** and **minority** as well as **obedience** to an authority figure.

Conformity and minority influence

The term 'conformity' refers to yielding (submitting) to the views of a majority. Research studies have shown how individuals can be influenced to conform to the views of majority groups (e.g. **Asch**) and to social norms (e.g. **Zimbardo**). **Minority social influence** occurs when a smaller group (or an individual) persuades a larger group to change its attitudes or behaviours. Minority influence may operate by means of converting majorities so that the effects, though slower to show, are more long-lasting than the effects of **majority influence**, where people may conform in public but not change their views in private.

Obedience to authority

Obedience refers to **complying with the requests or orders of someone in authority**. Many research studies have shown how readily people obey authority figures. **Milgram** carried out the first studies in obedience and his research has been accused of lacking validity. However, his studies have been replicated in other situations (e.g. **Hofling**) and in other countries (e.g. **Meeus and Raaijmakers**). The reasons proposed for people obeying include: gradual commitment; lapsing into an agentic state so that one no longer feels responsible for one's own actions; not wanting to cause a fuss by disobeying; having an authoritarian personality and therefore submitting to those in authority. People may **resist** pressures to obey if they retain a sense of personal responsibility, possess high levels of moral reasoning, see other people disobey or feel that they are being pressured too blatantly.

Critical issue: Ethical issues in psychological research

Ethical issues that concern research psychologists include the use of **deception**, obtaining **fully informed consent**, ensuring participants know they are **free to leave at any time** during the procedure and **protecting participants from harm**. Many ethical criticisms have been levelled against research in the area of social influence (particularly against Milgram's work), but some psychologists believe the importance of the issues researched outweighs the risk of harm to participants. Psychologists have developed **ethical guidelines** to provide a moral framework within which research is conducted. These guidelines are regularly revised to reflect changing social values.

Question for you to try

Examiner's hints
- Explain each of the three terms in part (a) **separately**. Each is marked independently.
- Take care that the procedures and findings you describe in part (b) are from the **same study**.
- Each of the outlines required in part (c) is worth 3 marks. Therefore, you will need to provide a **little more detail** for each of these than you gave for each of the three explanations in part (a).
- In part (d) you **do not have to refer directly to the quotation**.
- Remember that in part (d) you need to show your **skills in analysing and evaluating** the ethical objections raised against social influence research.

(a) Explain what is meant by the terms 'social influence', 'minority influence' and 'ethical issues'.   [2 marks + 2 marks + 2 marks]

(b) Describe the procedures *and* findings from **one** study of minority influence.
                                                                              [6 marks]

(c) Outline **two** ways in which minorities exert their influence.
                                                                    [3 marks + 3 marks]

(d) 'The controversy surrounding research by Milgram and Zimbardo was caused largely by the unpalatable nature of their findings: situations, not personal character, cause people to behave the way they do.'

To what extent are the ethical objections levelled against social influence research, such as that carried out by Milgram and Zimbardo, justified?
                                                                             [12 marks]

Answers are given on pp. 91–92.

Exam Questions

Time allowed: 45 minutes

Answer **both** questions. You should attempt all parts of these questions.

Question 1

In an attempt to test the anxiety-reducing properties of a new anti-anxiety drug *sedinex*, doctors prescribed the drug to 12 patients referred for job-related stress symptoms. A control group of 12 patients was prescribed a placebo (a pill that has no physiological effect) instead of *sedinex*. Participants were not aware that they were taking part in a clinical trial of the drug.

A number of physiological measurements were taken before treatment and after patients had been on their respective treatments for one week. Patients were also asked to keep a diary and rate how stressed they felt at the end of each working day (on a scale of 1 [not at all stressed] to 10 [extremely stressed]). Results for resting heart rate and subjective stress rating (how stressed the participants felt) are summarized in the graphs below.

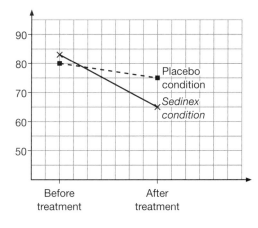

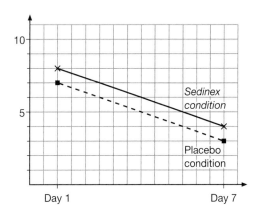

Figure 1 **Changes in mean resting heart rate before and after treatment**

Figure 2 **Changes in median stress ratings over one week of treatment**

(a) Suggest a suitable directional (one-tailed) hypothesis for this investigation.

[2 marks]

(b) Identify the independent variable used in this investigation.

[1 mark]

(c) Explain why it was considered necessary to use a control group that received only the placebo instead of *sedinex*. [2 marks]

(d) Why was it important for participants to keep a diary of their subjective stress ratings during the study? [2 marks]

(e) Using the information in Figure 1 and Figure 2, give **two** conclusions about the effectiveness of *sedinex* as an anti-anxiety drug. [2 marks + 2 marks]

(f) Describe **one** ethical issue that might have arisen in this investigation. [2 marks]

(g) Explain **one** way in which the design of this research might affect the validity of the results. [2 marks]

Question 2

In order to investigate possible gender differences in the aggressive behaviour of pre-school children, you and another student researcher are given access to a local playgroup to carry out observations of the children who attend there.

(a) Suggest an appropriate non-directional (two-tailed) hypothesis for this study. [2 marks]

(b) Explain how you might operationalize 'aggressive behaviour' in this study. [2 marks]

(c) Identify one possible source of investigator effect in this study, and explain how you might attempt to overcome it. [3 marks]

(d) Explain **two** advantages of using the naturalistic observation method in this study. [2 marks + 2 marks]

(e) Describe how you might check for reliability between the observations of the two researchers. [2 marks]

(f) Explain **one** reason why a pilot study might have been useful in this investigation. [2 marks]

(a) Suggest a suitable directional (one-tailed) hypothesis for this investigation. [2 marks]

HELENA'S ANSWER

The effect of sedinex will be greater than the effect of the placebo.

CHRIS'S ANSWER

Participants who take sedinex show less signs of anxiety after a week than those who take a placebo.

(b) Identify the independent variable used in this investigation. [1 mark]

HELENA'S ANSWER

The drug condition (sedinex or placebo).

CHRIS'S ANSWER

It is something that is manipulated by the researcher to see its effect on something else.

(c) Explain why it was considered necessary to use a control group that received only the placebo instead of *sedinex*. [2 marks]

HELENA'S ANSWER

It was necessary to use a control group that didn't receive sedinex because otherwise the researchers wouldn't know what had had the effect.

CHRIS'S ANSWER

The placebo condition helped the researchers to discount any effects that might have been due to participants simply believing that they were taking an anti-anxiety drug. If the drug really did have an effect, it should be greater than the effect shown by the placebo alone.

How to score full marks

Part (a)

 HELENA'S ANSWER

Helena's hypothesis does contain some of the essential ingredients for a directional hypothesis – it predicts a **causal relationship** between *sedinex* and, presumably, the amount of subsequent anxiety, and this is indeed stated **directionally**. However, **this is far too vague, and we are left filling in some of the details on Helena's behalf**. What **sort** of effect is being predicted here, and how would we know how to measure it? In technical terms, **Helena has failed to operationalize her dependent variable**. She should have specified the exact effect that *sedinex* would have (in this case, she might have said that it would lower heart rate, or make people feel less stressed). **Although she is on the right track with this hypothesis, it is too vague for the full 2 marks**.

 CHRIS'S ANSWER

Chris's hypothesis is much better. He has predicted a **causal** relationship between *sedinex* and signs of anxiety, and has stated that the experimental group will show fewer signs of anxiety (this is what makes it **directional**) than the control group (thus comparing the two conditions in the study). **By adding that this effect will be evident at the end of a week, he has also made it clear that he expects an experimental effect** as a result of taking the *sedinex*, and not one as a result of taking the placebo. His answer therefore scores the full 2 marks.

Part (b)

 HELENA'S ANSWER

Helena has correctly identified the independent variable as the drug condition that participants were placed in. She has elaborated on this by adding (in brackets) that she means the 'sedinex or placebo' conditions. **This is a good thing to do as it ensures full marks**.

 CHRIS'S ANSWER

Chris appears to have misunderstood the requirements of the question. He has **defined what an independent variable is rather than**, as asked for in the question, **what it is in this investigation**.

Part (c)

 HELENA'S ANSWER

Helena has provided an answer which is along the right lines. She is aware that a control group is there as a way of seeing whether the drug had an effect. There is a fair amount of 'assisted reading' going on here on Helena's behalf. What exactly does she mean by the phrase 'wouldn't know what had had the effect'? **It would have helped Helena if she could simply have added something along the lines of Chris's second sentence**. As it is, she scores only 1 mark. It is often frustrating for the examiner to find that students know a lot more, but simply fail to add this to their answer when they obviously have time to do so. It doesn't matter if your language is not as precise as Chris's, but **you should try to illuminate your answer with something that makes the meaning of your statement as clear as possible**.

 CHRIS'S ANSWER

Chris has done exactly that by explaining why a placebo condition was being used (to discount any effects due to participants believing they were receiving treatment) **and explaining how this would work in practice**. He tells us, quite rightly, that if the drug really did work, it should have more of an effect than the placebo alone. **This is a very effective answer so deserves both of the marks available**.

(d) Why was it important for participants to keep a diary of their subjective stress ratings during the study? [2 marks]

HELENA'S ANSWER

So the participants could keep a record of whether they felt differently over the week, as stress is all about what we feel as much as whether our body acts differently.

CHRIS'S ANSWER

Participants were asked to keep a record of their subjective stress ratings so these could be compared to the actual changes in resting heart rate over the same period. It is useful to have this extra information as change in heart rate alone may not be a reliable indicator of changes in stress levels.

(e) Using the information in Figure 1 and Figure 2, give **two** conclusions about the effectiveness of *sedinex* as an anti-anxiety drug. [2 marks + 2 marks]

HELENA'S ANSWER

The group that takes sedinex does better after a week than the group that takes the placebo,

but there isn't a lot of difference between the two groups in Figure 2.

CHRIS'S ANSWER

Figure 1 shows that the mean resting heart rate of the participants who have been taking sedinex drops significantly over the week's trial compared to the placebo condition.

Participants in the sedinex condition <u>and</u> those in the placebo condition feel less stressed after the week and there isn't a lot of difference in the levels of subjective stress ratings between the two groups.

(f) Describe **one** ethical issue that might have arisen in this investigation. [2 marks]

HELENA'S ANSWER

It is not ethical to withhold treatment (such as anti-anxiety drugs) from people who have need for them. This is wrong because it puts them at risk. Also it is wrong to deceive people in the placebo condition into thinking that they are taking a drug that will make them better when in fact they aren't.

CHRIS'S ANSWER

Participants were not given the opportunity to give their informed consent to take part in this study. Informed consent means having enough information to make a reasoned decision about taking part in a study.

(g) Explain **one** way in which the design of this research might affect the validity of the results. [2 marks]

HELENA'S ANSWER

One problem is that the participants may act differently because they know they are taking part in an experiment. For example, participants might not want to mess up the research by saying how they really feel.

CHRIS'S ANSWER

The research might have been affected by factors that are outside of the researcher's control (e.g. the amount of other stress experienced by the participants in the week they were taking the drug). This may have interfered with the accuracy of both the heart rate and stress ratings taken during the week.

How to score full marks

Part (d)

HELENA'S ANSWER

Helena is aware that **the gathering of stress ratings is important because they add an extra dimension to the measurement of stress**. She qualifies this by stating that 'stress is all about what we feel as much as whether our body acts differently'. **This is a sensible addition and guarantees the full two marks for this part of the question.** Although Helena would not lose any marks for the content in this answer, **she needs to write in complete sentences to make sure she does not lose any of the marks awarded for Quality of Written Communication (QoWC).**

CHRIS'S ANSWER

Chris has also seen the importance of gathering this extra bit of information during the study. **He is aware that subjective stress ratings could usefully be compared to the changes in resting heart rate** and qualifies this by explaining that heart rate may not be a **reliable** indicator of stress levels by itself. **Note that Chris has written in complete sentences so does not put his QoWC marks under threat.**

Part (e)

HELENA'S ANSWER

Helena has correctly interpreted the two graphs, but her interpretation is rather imprecise and lacking in detail. Figure 1 shows a fall in the resting heart rate of both groups, but this is more pronounced in the *sedinex* group than in the placebo group. **It isn't sufficient simply to say that one group 'does better' than the other, because 'better' isn't defined.** Likewise, for her second conclusion, Helena points out that there 'isn't a lot of difference' between the two groups, but doesn't explain in what way there isn't a difference. **She should have pointed out that there was little difference in terms of change in resting heart rate over the duration of the study.** It may seem obvious to you what you are talking about when using such imprecise phrases, but **the exact relationship should always be spelt out for maximum marks.** As it is, Helena's answer scores only 2 out of the possible 4 marks.

CHRIS'S ANSWER

Chris correctly points out that the mean resting heart rate 'drops significantly' over the week's trial 'compared' to the placebo condition. **Note that Chris's answer is far more precise. He states exactly what change is indicated in Figure 1** (i.e., change in the mean resting heart rate) and demonstrates this comparatively by stating the difference between the two conditions in this respect. **Chris's second conclusion takes account of the information in Figure 2 and again states the precise change** (in subjective stress ratings) over the week. This time he concludes that 'there isn't a lot of difference in the levels of subjective stress ratings between the two groups'. His answer deserves the full 4 marks.

Part (f)

HELENA'S ANSWER

Helena has clearly got her teeth into this question. **She is aware that the withholding of treatment from people who may need it is ethically unacceptable.** She qualifies this by suggesting that this may put them at risk. **This is fine for the 2 marks**, so there is **no need for the second issue** (of deception) that follows. **This simply wastes time that could be better employed elsewhere.**

 CHRIS'S ANSWER

Chris has suggested that participants may not have given their **informed consent** to take part in the study and goes on to explain what is meant by informed consent. **This is quite appropriate**, as we are told that the **participants were not aware that they were taking part in a clinical trial of the drug**, therefore, presumably, were not able to give their full **informed** consent. This is a difficult question to mark as the question does ask for an ethical issue that **might** arise. However, **it is always better to go for ethical issues that are obviously part of the study being described**.

Part (g)

HELENA'S ANSWER

Helena appears to be confused over the procedures used in this research, where participants are unaware of their involvement in a clinical manipulation. **Helena has compounded this misunderstanding with her choice of example**. We are actually told in the stimulus material for this study that participants did not know they were part of a clinical trial of the drug. **They would not, therefore, have adjusted their behaviour in the way suggested by Helena**. Her answer therefore earns no marks.

CHRIS'S ANSWER

Chris quite rightly explains that studies such as this are 'more likely to be affected by factors that are outside of the researcher's control'. **He has wisely qualified this by giving an example drawn from this study** (i.e., that participants may differ in the levels of stress they experienced in the week while taking the drug). He goes on to **explain** in what way this might affect the validity of the results. Chris's answer earns him the full 2 marks.

Don't forget ...

- **Make sure you read the question carefully** and **give no more and no less** than the question's actual requirements.

- **When asked for a description or explanation, provide some detail.** Giving examples (Chris does this a lot) may help to convince the examiner that you know what you are talking about.

- If you are asked to outline or describe **more than one** feature or explanation, **remember that each is marked independently**, so **don't spend too much time on one to the detriment of the other**.

- Unless you are merely asked to 'identify' or 'state' something (usually indicated by the award of 1 mark rather than 2 or 3), **you must write in complete sentences**. This contributes to your overall **Quality of Written Communication** (QoWC) mark.

Helena's answers to Question 2, parts (a) to (f)

In order to investigate possible gender differences in the aggressive behaviour of pre-school children, you and another student researcher are given access to a local playgroup to carry out observations of the children who attend there.

(a) Suggest an appropriate non-directional (two-tailed) hypothesis for this study. [2 marks]

(b) Explain how you might operationalize 'aggressive behaviour' in this study. [2 marks]

(c) Identify **one** possible source of investigator effect in this study, and explain how you might attempt to overcome it. [3 marks]

(d) Explain **two** advantages of using the naturalistic observation method in this study. [2 marks + 2 marks]

(e) Describe how you might check for reliability between the observations of the two researchers. [2 marks]

(f) Explain **one** reason why a pilot study might have been useful in this investigation. [2 marks]

> **A pity, quite an elegant hypothesis but this is *directional* rather than *non-directional*.**

(a) Pre-school boys display more aggressive behaviour when playing than do pre-school girls.

> **This is an appropriate way of operationalizing aggressive behaviour (although *verbal* aggression is also important).**

(b) Aggressive behaviour could be operationalized by counting the number of times that a child pushes or hits other children in the playgroup.

> **Correct identification of a possible source of investigator bias, although *solution a bit vague*.**

(c) Children may act differently because they are being watched by the researchers. They could overcome this by hiding so they couldn't be seen by the children.

> **The first advantage is rather vague and *not tied explicitly to this study*. The second advantage is wrong as this method does have potential ethical problems.**

(d) One advantage of using the naturalistic observation method is that behaviour tends to be more natural. A second advantage is that there are no ethical problems involved in studies that use this method (as there is no intrusion).

> **This is correct in principle, although Helena does not say exactly *how* observations would be compared to check for reliability.**

(e) The researchers could compare their observations to check if they are the same.

> **Good. A *full and accurate explanation* of why a pilot study might be useful.**

(f) A pilot study would be useful so that the researchers could check that they agree on what is and what is not aggressive behaviour so that when they do the study for real they are recording the same information.

Chris's answers to Question 2, parts (a) to (f)

A *good hypothesis*. It shows a clear relationship between gender and aggressive behaviour and is *non-directional*.

(a) Male and female pre-school children will show different levels of aggressive behaviour in their play activities. 2/2

A *very complete and precise explanation* with good use of examples to illustrate the answer.

(b) Researchers could decide on different categories of physical aggression (such as hitting another child) or verbal aggression (such as shouting at another child) and record every time a child performed that behaviour. 2/2

Chris has identified an appropriate source of investigator bias and explained fully how this might be overcome.

(c) Because the researchers are adults, the children may not behave as aggressively when being watched as they would normally. The researchers could use video cameras to record the children's behaviour. This would make the children less aware that they were being watched and so more likely to behave naturally. 3/3

The first advantage is explained fully *and* in the context of this study. The second is a more general advantage and needs to make reference to the behaviours studied in *this* investigation.

(d) Because children are in their own environment, they are more likely to act as they would normally, therefore any observations are more likely to be valid. 2/2 Naturalistic observation enables researchers to study behaviour in more depth compared to what is possible in a laboratory study. 1/2

Chris has stated the *type of reliability* being checked. This helps him to provide a more *focused* description, illustrated by an *appropriate* example.

(e) One way of checking for inter-observer reliability is to use a video recording and check to see if both researchers are recording the same behaviours as aggressive behaviour. For example, one may see a behaviour as 'aggressive' whereas the other may see it as 'mucking about'. 2/2

Again, Chris has made good use of the time available and has provided a *full explanation*, accompanied by a very useful *example*.

(f) A pilot study would be useful in this investigation because it gives researchers a chance to try out all their techniques in advance, and check that there are no problems (such as the reaction of the children to being observed) that will affect the study when it is carried out later. 2/2

Key points to remember

Experiments

The **laboratory experiment** gives the experimenter greater ability to **control and alter the variables being tested**. Because of this, the experimenter can eliminate many extraneous variables that might otherwise affect the results. In the **field experiment**, participants are **not aware that they are taking part in an experiment**. This replaces the artificial setting of the laboratory with a more natural one. The **natural experiment** is not regarded as a true experiment because **the independent variable is not under the control of the experimenter** and it is not possible to exert control over the allocation of participants to conditions.

Investigations using correlational analysis

Correlational analyses yield **graphical and mathematical representations** of the degree and direction of relatedness of two sets of measurements. This can be achieved through **scattergrams** and through **correlation coefficients**. Knowledge of the degree and direction of any relationship enables us to predict (with varying degrees of certainty) a value of one variable if we know the value of the other. **Correlations can be used when experiments are inappropriate or impossible, but do not tell us anything about causality.**

Questionnaire surveys

These are techniques whereby **the investigator makes use of a structured set of questions to obtain information about a particular area**. Questions can be **fixed-choice**, where respondents can only choose from a fixed set of options, or **open-ended**, where respondents can say whatever they like. Surveys tend to be an **economical method of gathering a lot of information** from a lot of people, **but their effectiveness may be limited by poor design**, such as the use of leading or ambiguous questions.

Naturalistic observations

Naturalistic observations take place in the **natural setting in which we would normally observe a particular behaviour**. The researcher does not attempt to manipulate any aspect of the situation, but merely observes (although people may react to the presence of the observer). Such observations may yield more natural behaviour (compared to investigations in the laboratory) and may produce greater insights because of the longer period of observation. **Because the observer has no control over an independent variable, no conclusions about cause and effect are possible**.

Interviews

Interviews typically involve **face-to-face interaction between the interviewer and the interviewee**. Interviews may be **highly structured** (in terms of the questions asked) or **unstructured**. The former may involve a more objective form of interviewing, whereas the more flexible and searching unstructured interview may be a rich source of **qualitative** data. Interviewers are trained to deliver questions without bias or encouragement to interviewees to answer them in a certain way. **If interviewers cannot develop an appropriate rapport with their interviewees, then questions may not be answered in an open and honest manner**.

Question 1

In order to investigate whether there is a relationship between extraversion (a personality dimension characterized by greater impulsiveness and sociability) and self-confidence, a psychologist takes a random sample of 10 male participants from a school sixth form. After measuring both extraversion and self-confidence in her sample, the psychologist constructs the scattergram shown in Figure 1.

(a) State the main aim of this investigation. [1 mark]

(b) State a suitable null hypothesis for this investigation. [2 marks]

(c) Describe **one** advantage and **one** disadvantage of correlational analyses such as this. [2 marks + 2 marks]

(d) Explain what is meant by 'random sampling', and describe how a random sample might have been taken in this study. [2 marks + 2 marks]

(e) Explain the difference between a positive correlation and a negative correlation. [2 marks]

(f) Describe the relationship between extraversion and self-confidence as shown in Figure 1. [2 marks]

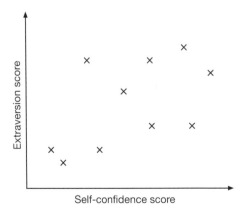

Figure 1 **Scattergram of relationship between extraversion and self-confidence**

Question 2

A researcher has been given permission by an eating disorders support group to interview five teenage girls who are recovering from anorexia nervosa. She is particularly interested in how each of these girls explains the reasons why they suffered from this disorder.

(a) What would be the main aim of this study? [1 mark]

(b) Give **one** reason why an interview would be the best method to use for this type of investigation. [2 marks]

(c) Explain how the researcher might take her sample for this study. [2 marks]

(d) Describe **one** ethical issue in this study and explain how this might be dealt with. [2 marks + 2 marks]

(e) Give **one** way in which the relationship between the researcher and participants might influence the results, and explain how this effect might be minimized. [2 marks + 2 marks]

(f) Give **one** way that the qualitative data from these interviews might be analysed. [2 marks]

Answers are given on pp. 93–95.

Chapter 1 Memory

🎯 How to score full marks

(a) Working memory consists of several slave-systems that can work independently from one another under the control of the central executive. This key component of the model acts like a planner and it co-ordinates the distribution and collection of information from its slave-systems as well as from LTM. It can handle information from any sensory modality, but its storage capacity is limited. The slave-systems have specific roles and all have restricted capacity. The phonological loop acts like an inner voice and allows rehearsal of verbal items and has a duration of approx. 2 seconds. The visuo-spatial scratchpad acts like an inner eye and is responsible for processing visual stimuli such as a tracking task. A later addition to the model was the primary acoustic store, which acts as an inner ear and can process non-verbal sounds.

> **Examiner's comment**
>
> **All the main features of the model are described here.** Note how the use of **succinct terms** such as 'sensory modality', 'visual stimuli', 'tracking task' and 'non-verbal sounds' allows you to cut down on unnecessary words – you do not have to explain these terms to the examiner. Note also that it is not necessary to write about the effectiveness of the model.

(b) One study on the duration of STM was carried out by Peterson and Peterson. They gave their participants brief, visual presentations of consonant trigrams (e.g. BXQ). After the trigram had disappeared from the screen, the participants were given a number (e.g. 109) and asked to count backwards in threes. This was to stop them repeating the trigram to themselves. The experimenters stopped them after intervals ranging from 3 to 18 seconds and then asked them to recall the trigram. They found that the percentage of trigrams correctly recalled became progressively poorer the longer rehearsal was prevented. After only 3 seconds delay, recall had declined even though 3 items should normally be well within the digit span. After 18 seconds, recall fell below 10%.

Conrad carried out a study into encoding in STM. He showed participants a set of capital letters on a screen and asked them to write them down in the order that they had appeared. The letters were presented very quickly, so participants had to rely on their STM to hold them for long enough to write them down. Conrad had two conditions – one condition contained a set of letters that sound similar when they are said out loud, e.g. P, V, B, D, T etc., and the other condition consisted of letters that do not sound the same, e.g. K, Z, M, X, F. Even though he only presented sets that were within the digit span (e.g. 7 letters or less), participants consistently recalled fewer letters in the acoustically similar condition than in the acoustically dissimilar condition.

> **Examiner's comment**
>
> Two appropriate studies have been described, although there are others which are equally suitable, for example Baddeley's study on acoustic coding. The candidate has clearly indicated which study is about duration and which is about encoding. Both **procedure** and **findings** have been **accurately described** in the two studies. Note that it is not necessary to give equal weighting to the procedures and the findings for full marks. It will often be the case that there is more to say about one aspect of a study than another. The important point is that you **address both requirements**, i.e., you describe both the procedures and the findings, even if you do not write exactly the same amount for each. However, note that **each study** is marked independently out of 6 marks, so **spend about the same amount of time on describing each.**

(c) One reason why witnesses might be unreliable is that they reconstruct their memory for events in line with previously stored knowledge. Bartlett, in his 'War of the Ghosts' study, for example, showed that people changed the details of the original story in order to make it more consistent with their own experience. However, his research is criticized for being poorly controlled and Gauld and Stephenson found that people could recall stories accurately if they were led to believe that accuracy was very important. Foster also found that accuracy was greater for a group of participants who believed that their testimony was to be used in a genuine case than for a group who knew that they were simply taking part in an experiment. This highlights the problems of applying laboratory results to real-life situations.

Loftus has shown in a number of studies that people can be influenced by misleading post-event information. For example, she showed participants slides depicting the events leading up to a car accident and then asked them questions in which she included some false information about the nature of a road sign. Participants fed the misleading information were later more likely to pick the wrong slide in a recognition test. She also found that the tendency to pick the wrong slide persisted even when participants were promised money as a reward for accurate recognition. This made her think that the original event had been deleted from memory and replaced by the inaccurate version. Evidence from the cognitive interview technique suggests that this is not the case. Eyewitnesses can be reliable if the correct cues are provided, which suggests that the original information is still available.

Loftus herself found that there is a limit to how much witnesses can be misled by false information. She found that participants correctly recalled the colour of a stolen purse (red) even though they had been fed later information from a respectable source (a professor) that the purse was brown. So, it looks as though key elements that stand out are less likely to be distorted than things that are less central.

In one study on weapon focus, Loftus found that anxiety about the weapon detracted attention from other details such as the attacker's face etc. and so led to lower reliability. However, Christianson and Hubinette found that, in real-life situations, fear actually heightens accuracy. It seems, then, that laboratory experiments might give a false picture of the extent of eyewitness unreliability.

Examiner's comment

This material is **clearly focused on the question** and makes a good attempt at evaluating relevant psychological research. Although the question asks for the extent of **support** for the idea that eyewitness testimony is unreliable, it is **important to give both sides of the argument.** It does not matter which side of the argument is eventually more convincing, provided that you discuss both. The quotation is provided to help you establish a context for your answer. You do not have to refer to it at all and, in this question, you do not have to write exclusively about Loftus. A range of studies has been used effectively to make clear evaluative points. Note that it is not necessary to include long descriptions of research studies. This will waste time and not gain you any marks. **You should only include as much procedural detail as is necessary to draw an appropriate conclusion.** You have a very limited time to answer this question (approximately 12 minutes), so you will have to be selective. The example given above is only one way of tackling the question. It could have been successfully answered using different examples of research, e.g. more evidence based on schema theory or evidence from face recognition studies. The main thing to remember is that this question gives you the opportunity to show your ability to **analyse and evaluate psychological research (AO2).**

🎯 How to score full marks

(a) *Maternal deprivation* refers to the situation where a young child is separated from and thereby deprived of the love of its primary caregiver, usually its mother. Bowlby claimed that when this occurred the child's ability to form relationships in the future would be detrimentally affected.

Privation refers to the lack (rather than the loss) of something. For example, when a child never has the chance to form an attachment because no attachment figure is available.

Secure attachment refers to the strong, contented bond that a child has with its primary caregiver. A securely attached infant uses the mother figure as a safe base for exploration, is distressed when separated from her but easily comforted when she returns.

> **Examiner's comment**
>
> **All three terms are explained in appropriate detail.** You do not have to provide exactly the same length of answer for each as long as you have given a clear explanation.

(b) Robertson and Bowlby (1952) observed short-term effects of separation in children placed in residential nurseries because their mothers had to be away. The children showed three progressive reactions. First, they cried and called for their mothers (protest stage). Then they became apathetic, only cried occasionally and lost interest in their surroundings (despair phase). Finally, in the detachment stage, they appeared to recover and take more of an interest, but when the mother returned they were not interested in her.

The main conclusion from this study was that young children should not be separated from their mothers if at all possible. Where separation is unavoidable the child's emotional needs must be catered for as well as their physical needs. Children should be prepared sensitively to help them cope with the separation, e.g. visiting where they will be staying and meeting the people who will be looking after them.

Tizard and Hodges looked at the long-term effects for children who had suffered maternal privation by being raised in an institution till they were 4 years old. Twenty-four of the children were adopted at age 4 and at ages 8 and 16 were found to be happy and attached to their adoptive parents. Fifteen children were restored to their natural homes, but they did less well. Both groups of children had problems in school, craving adult attention and finding it difficult to make friends.

The conclusions drawn from this study are that early detrimental effects of institutional care can be remedied if there is an opportunity to form attachments later. The adoptive parents were very loving and eager to have the children, but some of the birth families were not happy about having children returned to them. Some privation effects, however, were long-lasting, as shown by the difficulties the children found in school where their teachers and classmates may not have made allowances for the children's early disadvantages.

> **Examiner's comment**
>
> **Two appropriate studies are described** with **both findings and conclusions given for each.** It is a good idea to make it clear when you are writing about the findings and when writing about the conclusions. Don't leave the examiners to work it out for themselves. Other equally appropriate studies you could have chosen include that by Robertson and Robertson (1971). They showed that with suitable preparation a child could adjust successfully to separation from its mother in the short term. The case studies of isolated and abused children such as Genie

(Curtiss, 1977) and the Czech twin boys (Koluchova, 1976) would also have been appropriate for this answer.

(c)   The term 'day care' refers to the care of pre-school children by people other than the children's parents. Some research has shown that both the cognitive and social development of a child may be enhanced by the stimulation provided by a nursery or playgroup. Andersson (1992) studied Swedish children and found that those who had received day care before 1 year old performed better academically and socially than those who had stayed at home. However, we have to be cautious about interpreting these findings. The 'day care' children in this study came from families with a higher socio-economic status than the children who stayed home. Their privileged background, therefore, might explain their better school performance.

A study in Texas, however, found that children who experienced day care did less well when they went to school. Perhaps the reason for the different findings lies in the different support offered for day care by the two countries. In Sweden, high-quality day care is well financed and regulated. In Texas, however, the care is probably less good as state regulations are less strict. Therefore, we see that in order to evaluate the benefits of day care we have to consider the home backgrounds of the children who are receiving the care and the quality of care offered.

Some children appear to benefit from day care more than others. Egeland and Hiester found that insecurely attached children benefited more from day care than securely attached children, presumably because they needed the extra help and attention to compensate for what was lacking at home.

At present, some care provided by childminders has been shown to be more concerned with keeping children quiet than enhancing their development (Bryant et al.), and so it seems that stimulating resources and high-quality staff may be important factors in determining whether day care is beneficial. According to Schaffer, high-quality care can be achieved by having a low turnover of well-trained staff and low child–staff ratios to permit rewarding interactions between children and carers.

On balance, the evidence supports the claim that quality day care benefits those who receive it, especially those who may lack opportunities at home. Therefore the focus of attention should now be on how to improve the care on offer.

Examiner's comment

All the information given in this answer is focused on the question set. The findings of relevant empirical studies are evaluated as a means of addressing the question. Because of time constraints, it is inevitable that only a limited number of evaluative points can be covered. This is OK, but you need to **select relevant points that enable you to show your evaluative skills to best effect.** You may have noticed that the answer does not refer directly to the quotation, nor is this required by the question. Remember that **2 marks are allocated for the quality of written communication** shown in a paper. It is worthwhile trying to write clearly and accurately, using specialist terms correctly.

🎯 How to score full marks

(a) Under conditions of arousal, the pituitary gland releases adrenocorticotrophic hormone (ACTH) into the bloodstream. This travels to the adrenal cortex, which releases corticosteroids. These mobilize energy resources and maintain blood flow and heart rate to get oxygen to the muscles that may be needed in a 'fight or flight' response.

During arousal, the sympathetic division of the autonomic nervous system stimulates the adrenal medulla to release the hormones adrenaline and noradrenaline into the bloodstream. These hormones, in conjunction with corticosteroids, reinforce sympathetic arousal by stimulating heart rate and mobilizing further energy resources in the body. This enables the body to deal with the stressor by activating a 'fight or flight' response.

> **Examiner's comment**
>
> The outline of two ways in which the body responds to stress (pituitary-adrenal cortex and sympathetic-adrenal medulla activity) are **accurate and detailed.** You are only asked for the ways that the **body** responds, so there is **no need for elaborate introductions or unnecessary detail** about the nature of the stressor.

(b) The immune system protects the body from disease organisms and other foreign bodies, known as antigens. Research studies have generally found that short-term stress (such as marital arguments) can lead to suppression of the immune system, whilst long-term stress may lead to parallel long-term reduction in immune function (Willis et al., 1987).

Research by Glaser et al. (1992) showed that under conditions of stress, the levels of adrenaline and noradrenaline increase, and these increases can suppress aspects of immune function, including killer T cells (cells that attack antigens). This suppression then raises the risk of viral infection. McEwan and Stellar (1993), for example, found that colds and other infections are more likely to occur on weekends after busy and stressful weekdays at work.

> **Examiner's comment**
>
> This answer provides a **focused outline of research studies** rather than a more general account of the different ways in which immune system functioning might be affected by stress. There are three research studies quoted by name (and date). Although names and dates are not **required**, it is a good idea to **include** them as it makes describing the source of your insights that much easier. There is a lot of other relevant research that you could use in response to this question, including the work carried out by Janice Kiecolt-Glaser and colleagues. The description is both **accurate and detailed**, and is a very effective use of the six minutes allocated for this answer.

(c) Johansson et al. (1978) studied workers in a Swedish sawmill, comparing the stress levels of 'finishers' (who finished the timber as the last stage of the process) with other workers in the sawmill. They recorded workers' levels of stress hormones at various intervals during workdays and rest days, and looked at patterns of absenteeism and sickness.

They concluded that the work environment of the 'finishers' made them particularly vulnerable to stress. They were responsible for the wages of the whole factory, their job was highly skilled but monotonous and repetitive, and the job was machine paced (giving them no control over the pace of the work).

(d) The role of control in the experience of stress is supported by the Whitehall studies (Marmot et al., 1998). These studies found a dramatic difference in perceived stress between those at the top of the Civil Service hierarchy and those at the bottom. This demonstrated that there is a social gradient in stress-related illness, determined by an individual's position in the hierarchy, with those at the bottom being more vulnerable to stress-related illnesses than those at the top.

It is possible that these differences might be explainable by lifestyle, but even after adjustments for risk factors such as diet, physical activity and social support, the difference still existed. Marmot et al. concluded that the major difference between individuals at the bottom of the hierarchy and those at the top was in the degree of perceived control over their life. The lower the position in the hierarchy, the less the opportunity to influence events causing the stress.

The importance of control in reducing the experience of stress can also be shown in studies where the individual's control over the source of the stress is illusory. Work by Glass and Singer (1972) found that if two groups of people were exposed to an uncontrollable noise, the group who were given a button to press (even though it had no effect on the noise) showed a smaller stress response than those simply exposed to the noise.

The importance of control over longer periods has also been demonstrated in studies of learned helplessness. Seligman (1975) showed that participants exposed to uncontrollable noise later showed poor performance in tasks where they *could* control the noise. The experience of life as uncontrollable is stressful and an important aspect in the development of psychological depression (Seligman, 1975).

How to score full marks

(a) One problem with this definition concerns the concept of desirability. Many people would agree that one purpose of defining abnormality is to identify behaviours, which are undesirable and potentially harmful for the individual concerned, so that help can be given. If you define abnormality purely in terms of statistical infrequency, you would include things such as exceptionally high intelligence or courage or creativity. These are not thought to be undesirable and do not need treatment.

Another problem is that some types of behaviour which are seen as psychologically abnormal (e.g. depression and anxiety) are not particularly rare. For example, a recent large-scale survey found that almost half the people who responded had experienced a psychological disorder at some point in their life.

> **Examiner's comment**
> Two appropriate limitations of the statistical infrequency definition are given and they are clearly separated into two paragraphs. **Note that you do not have to write exactly the same amount for both, provided that you explain each one clearly.** It is useful, but not absolutely necessary, to give examples to illustrate your answer. Other limitations would have been just as acceptable, e.g. the gender and cultural issues that can affect statistical data. Note that you **do not have to waste time explaining what is meant by the term 'statistical infrequency'**.

(b) Freud believed that psychological disorders were caused by unresolved conflicts and anxieties from childhood that were pushed into the unconscious. Therefore, according to his psychodynamic model, treatment should be directed at helping clients to gain access to their unconscious mind and to face up to their repressed feelings. Since the unconscious is, by definition, not available to conscious awareness, Freud found ways to uncover it. For example, he analysed client dreams, which he called 'the royal road' to the unconscious, and he used free association where clients are encouraged to say whatever comes into their mind. Treatment can take a long time because of the difficulties involved in uncovering the unconscious. Since it is painful to face up to repressed memories, clients sometimes experience resistance. However, the ultimate goal of psychodynamic therapy is for the client to achieve insight. If clients can understand what has happened in their past, the idea is that they are more likely to be able to come to terms with what is going on in their lives now.

The medical model is based on the idea that psychological disorders have underlying physical causes and so it follows that the treatment associated with this model involves physical procedures. One assumption is that disorders can be caused by a chemical imbalance and that drugs can be used to counteract this. Drugs can be effective in alleviating the symptoms of some psychological disorders, but they can cause side-effects which are sometimes more troublesome than the disorder itself. While chemotherapy is probably the most widely used treatment, other biological interventions such as ECT and psychosurgery are also sometimes used. All these treatments are similar in that they interfere directly with bodily processes and their effects can be irreversible. Since the effects can be so serious, they can only be authorized by medically qualified practitioners. On the whole, these treatments offer relief from symptoms rather than a complete cure.

(c) Cross-cultural research suggests that eating disorders are more common in societies where slimness is valued. Even within such societies, certain groups e.g. ballet dancers are more prone to anorexia than others (Garner). Such findings lend support to behaviourists who think that eating disorders arise through conditioning or modelling. However, cross-cultural research can be difficult to interpret and low rates of diagnosis may simply reflect reluctance to report such disorders. It is also hard for behaviourists to explain why dieting continues after 'slimness' has been achieved.

Fairburn found that people with anorexia and bulimia were more perfectionist and self-denigrating than controls. This supports the cognitive explanation of distorted thinking patterns. However, the model does not explain where the distorted ideas come from in the first place. They could be the result rather than the cause of the disorder.

The psychodynamic model offers several explanations related to experiences in childhood. As a result of a survey of patients attending an eating disorder clinic, McClelland concluded that the repressed trauma of early sexual abuse emerges later as an eating disorder. However, people with eating disorders do not all have histories of abuse. Other psychodynamic explanations are linked to fears about sexual maturity, for example an association of fatness with pregnancy. This is a less convincing explanation of bulimia and, in any case, does not account for anorexia in boys.

Since no single psychological explanation seems to be adequate, it has been suggested that biology plays a part. Using twin studies, Holland found evidence for genetic transmission. Ward, however, found that environmental factors were better predictors of eating disorders. Other biological explanations include malfunction of the hypothalamus or of certain neurotransmitters, but there is little conclusive evidence and it is hard to disentangle cause from effect.

Eating disorders are complex and it seems likely that both psychological and biological factors contribute to their origins and maintenance.

Examiner's comment

This material is **focused on the question from the outset and includes reference to various psychological explanations for eating disorders**. The question requires you to put forward the case for psychological explanations of eating disorders, but it is helpful as part of your evaluation to contrast such explanations with those arising from the biological model. **You do not have much time to write your answer, so do not spend it on lengthy descriptions of the various explanations.** The focus should be on assessing the adequacy of such explanations and you can do this by providing evidence for and against them. Because of time restraints, **you will have to be selective** in the number and nature of the evaluative points you make. There are many other studies and/or examples that you could have used effectively in this answer – the choice is up to you, **provided that the points are all relevant and meet the requirements of the question.** It is important to remember that the question refers to 'eating disorders' and not simply to anorexia nervosa. You might find that you know more about possible causal explanations for anorexia, but make sure that you include some references to bulimia as well. You may have noticed that the answer does not refer directly to the quotation, nor is this required for full marks. The quotation is provided simply to point you in the right direction. Remember that there are two marks on each paper for the quality of written communication. It is worthwhile trying to write clearly and accurately and to use specialist terms correctly.

🎯 How to score full marks

(a) *Social influence* is the way in which another person or group of people may affect the attitudes or behaviours of an individual.

Minority influence refers to the effect of a persuasive smaller group or individual (minority) changing the attitudes or behaviours of a larger group (majority).

Ethical issues are the concerns that psychologists have about what is right or acceptable in the way they carry out their research, e.g. whether or not it is ever acceptable to deceive participants about the true nature of an experiment.

> **Examiner's comment**
>
> **All three terms are clearly explained.** You do not have to provide exactly the same length of answer for each as long as you have given a clear explanation.

(b) In one of Moscovici's studies the procedure involved asking 6 participants to judge the colour of 36 slides projected onto a screen. All slides were blue but some were brighter than others. Two participants, accomplices of the experimenter, called the slides 'green' either on all the 36 trials (consistent condition) or on 24 trials (inconsistent). The results were that in the consistent condition the genuine participants called the slides 'green' (went along with the minority view) in just over 8 per cent of trials. In the inconsistent condition, they yielded on only 1 per cent of trials.

> **Examiner's comment**
>
> **Both procedures and findings** of this well-known study of minority influence are **accurately described.** Other appropriate studies that could have been described include Clark's study of *Twelve Angry Men* or Nemeth's variation on Moscovici's experiment. It is a good idea to make it clear when you are writing about the procedures and when writing about the findings. Don't leave the examiner to work it out.

(c) Consistent minorities are more likely to be influential than minorities who are inconsistent. Members of a consistent minority do not contradict each other and they present a clear, coherent message. Consistency makes minorities appear genuine and worth listening to. This makes them more noticeable and so the majority begins to pay more attention to their views.

Another way that minorities exert influence is by showing commitment, i.e. being willing to make sacrifices if necessary. For example, members of the civil rights movement in the US and the suffragette movement in the UK were willing to go to prison. Gradually, respect for the minority views grows and the majority is converted.

> **Examiner's comment**
>
> **Two relevant ways** in which minorities exert their influence are outlined. Other ways are by showing flexibility and being in line with social trends. Make it clear when you move from outlining one point to outlining another.

(d) The use of deception, insufficient informed consent and failure to safeguard participants, perhaps causing them long-term psychological harm, are some of the ethical objections levelled against research in the area of social influence.

Milgram certainly deceived his participants about the true nature of his research, but he claimed this was necessary if obedience was to be researched properly. His critics argue that other methods, such as participants role-playing the situation, could be used instead. Others disagree, stating that the only way to find out the truth about how people behave in obedience situations is to place them in a real situation where obedience is asked of them, not by asking them to pretend! If this is so, then you cannot fully inform participants of the true nature of the study first.

Both Milgram and Zimbardo are accused of causing lasting harm to their participants by causing them to face unpleasant truths about themselves (e.g. giving 450 volts to someone). Milgram answered that he did not expect to find such high levels of obedience, especially since a preliminary survey showed that few people thought anyone normal would give high levels of shocks. Therefore, he could not have predicted the discomfort that many of the participants experienced. Nevertheless, he did carry on repeating his procedures many times with variations. But, by doing this, he found out what aspects of situations caused people to obey most readily. These are important discoveries.

Both Milgram and Zimbardo have responded to their critics by claiming thorough debriefing processes so that the participants left the laboratory feeling OK about themselves. Milgram also sent questionnaires to his participants and had some of them psychologically assessed. None reported any long-term ill effects, but maybe they still saw themselves as part of a study and influenced by demand characteristics.

Psychologists today are still divided as to whether the ethical objections to social influence research are valid or not. Some (e.g. Baumrind) believe that it is wrong to deceive people or to take any risks with their well-being. Others think that the importance of the topics being studied justified the slight risk posed to those who participated. Zimbardo proposes more (but better supervised) research be carried out to investigate these issues.

Examiner's comment

All the information given in this answer is focused on the question set. Three important ethical objections are identified concisely at the start, and each is then evaluated with reference to Milgram's and/or Zimbardo's research. The second, third and fourth paragraphs provide points for and against the ethical objections (i.e. evaluative, AO2, material). The answer concludes by giving two current views about the ethics of social influence research. Because of time constraints, it is inevitable that only a limited number of evaluative points can be covered. This is OK, but you need to **select relevant points that enable you to show your evaluative skills to best effect.** You may have noticed that the answer does not refer directly to the quotation, nor is this required by the question. However, the importance of situations in producing obedience is commented on in the answer given. The quotation is provided only to help you establish a context for your answer. **It is the question itself you must answer.**

🎯 How to score full marks

Question 1

(a) The aim of this investigation is to see if there is a correlational relationship between extraversion and self-confidence.

> **Examiner's comment**
>
> Questions such as this often fox students because they cannot believe that the aim can simply be the relationship stated in the question. **Sometimes, as here, a mark is given for spotting the aim in amongst the rest of the stimulus material.** This is fine (it also mentions the specific type of relationship being investigated, which is a good idea), and gets the mark available.

(b) There is no relationship between extraversion and self-confidence.

> **Examiner's comment**
>
> The null hypothesis stated above states that the data (in this case shown by the correlational relationship) do not vary in the way predicted by an alternative hypothesis. **The answer mentions the two variables** (extraversion and self-confidence) and **states clearly that there is no relationship between them, so is sufficient for full marks.**

(c) One advantage of a correlational analysis is that it provides valuable information about both the strength and direction of any relationship between two variables. One disadvantage is that a correlational analysis does not tell the researcher about any possible causal relationship between the two variables, only whether they are related in some way.

> **Examiner's comment**
>
> **This answer contains a clear and accurate description of an advantage and a disadvantage of correlational analyses.** In this question there was no need to place this advantage and disadvantage in the context of this study, **but be careful,** as sometimes this may be a requirement of the question set.

(d) Random sampling is a technique for selecting members from a target population so that each member of that population has an equal chance of being selected. One way of selecting a random sample in this study would have been to draw lots. The researcher could write every male member of the sixth form's name on a piece of paper and draw out 10 names.

> **Examiner's comment**
>
> **This is a precise definition of random sampling.** It is particularly good because it avoids simply regurgitating the words 'random' and 'sample'. Some students merely describe random sampling as a 'sample taken randomly' which **would not receive any marks as it merely recycles the same words.** This definition would receive full marks. There are many ways to take a random sample, and this one is perfectly appropriate for smallish populations and samples. Note that the answer makes reference to the 'target population' as being every male member of the school sixth form. As the sample is male we must assume, under the terms of a 'random' sample, that the target population must also be male. This also receives full marks.

(e) A positive correlation indicates that high values of one variable are matched by high values of the other, whereas a negative correlation indicates that high scores on one variable are matched by low scores on the other.

> **Examiner's comment**
>
> **This is accurate and the neat use of the word 'whereas' links the two forms of correlation together** so that a difference between them is evident. It gets full marks.

(f) Figure 1 shows a weak positive correlation between extraversion and self-confidence.

> **Examiner's comment**
>
> This interpretation has demonstrated an understanding of both the **strength** (weak) and **direction** (positive) between extraversion and self-confidence. This gets full marks.

Question 2

(a) The main aim of this study is to discover how people who have experienced anorexia nervosa explain the reasons for their former disorder.

> **Examiner's comment**
>
> **This is an accurate and succinct statement** of the aim, so receives full marks.

(b) The interview has the potential for flexible questioning so that responses concerning the origins of interviewees' anorexia can be explored in more detailed and personally relevant ways.

> **Examiner's comment**
>
> The interview does indeed have the potential for flexible questioning so is ideal for complex and sensitive issues such as anorexia.

(c) The most appropriate sampling method to use in this study would be an opportunity sample. A letter could be sent to each of the girls identified by the support group giving full details of the study and asking if they would consider volunteering to take part.

> **Examiner's comment**
>
> **This answer demonstrates a good understanding of why opportunity sampling is the most appropriate method to be used here,** and stresses the need for both informed consent and volunteer status.

(d) An important ethical issue is confidentiality. Participants have the right to expect that their responses will not be made public and that every effort is made to safeguard their identity. In this study, the names and any personal details that might be a clue to identity can be changed and participants can be told in advance those details of their responses that will be available for public scrutiny.

> **Examiner's comment**
>
> There are a number of ethical issues associated with interviews such as this. These include informed consent and competence to perform such sensitive interviews as well as confidentiality as described here. **This is an accurate and well-detailed description of what confidentiality means for this particular study and this is accompanied by a full account of how this could be achieved.**

(e) It is possible that participants would be reluctant to 'open up' on sensitive issues before they felt they could trust the interviewer. This might lead to superficial responses and would tell the investigator very little of interest. In order to minimize this effect, the interviewer could spend time prior to the interview gaining the trust of the interviewee, including assuring them that their responses would remain anonymous.

> **Examiner's comment**
>
> It is important in situations such as this to develop a sense of trust between interviewer and interviewee. Without this, as this answer suggests, responses may be at a superficial level. **There is a good account of how this trust might be achieved together with a concrete suggestion – assuring anonymity of responses.**

(f) It would be possible to identify themes in the responses of participants and link these to underlying psychological theories of anorexia. For example, reference to images of females in the media might be linked to the cognitive explanation of anorexia.

> **Examiner's comment**
>
> Analysing qualitative data can be complex and looking for **themes** (such as mentions of media images) in the interviewees' answers is an appropriate place to start. The answer qualifies this by adding that **these can then be linked to underlying theories about the origins of anorexia**. The use of an **example** certainly helps here.

Published by HarperCollins*Publishers* Limited
77–85 Fulham Palace Road
London W6 8JB

www.**Collins**Education.com
On-line support for schools and colleges

© HarperCollins*Publishers* Ltd 2001

First published 2001

ISBN 0 00 710747 1

Mike Cardwell, Claire Meldrum and Jane Willson assert the moral right to be identified as the authors of this work.

British Library Cataloguing in Publication Data
A catalogue record for this book is available from the British Library

Edited by Brigitte Lee
Picture research by Ginny Stroud-Lewis
Production by Kathryn Botterill
Cover design by Susi Martin-Taylor
Book design by Gecko Limited
Printed and bound at Scotprint, Haddington

Acknowledgements

Illustrations
Cartoon Artwork – Roger Penwill
DTP Artwork – Geoff Ward

Photographs
The Authors and Publisher are grateful to the following for permission to reproduce photographs:
© Bettmann/CORBIS 56; © Howard Davies/CORBIS 67; Sheena Verdun Taylor 20, 32, 44, 79

Every effort has been made to contact the holders of copyright material, but if any have been inadvertently overlooked, the Publishers will be pleased to make the necessary arrangements at the first opportunity.

You might also like to visit:
www.**fire**and**water**.com
The book lover's website